EVOLVE

STUDENT'S BOOK

with Digital Pack

Lindsay Clandfield, Ben Goldstein,
Ceri Jones, and Philip Kerr

2

CAMBRIDGE
UNIVERSITY PRESS

CAMBRIDGE
UNIVERSITY PRESS & ASSESSMENT

Shaftesbury Road, Cambridge CB2 8EA, United Kingdom

One Liberty Plaza, 20th Floor, New York, NY 10006, USA

477 Williamstown Road, Port Melbourne, VIC 3207, Australia

314–321, 3rd Floor, Plot 3, Splendor Forum, Jasola District Centre, New Delhi – 110025, India

103 Penang Road, #05-06/07, Visioncrest Commercial, Singapore 238467

Cambridge University Press & Assessment is a department of the University of Cambridge.

We share the University's mission to contribute to society through the pursuit of education, learning and research at the highest international levels of excellence.

www.cambridge.org
Information on this title: www.cambridge.org/9781009231794

First published with Digital Pack 2022

20 19 18 17

Printed in Malaysia by Vivar Printing

A catalogue record for this publication is available from the British Library

ISBN 978-1-009-23170-1 Student's Book with eBook
ISBN 978-1-009-23179-4 Student's Book with Digital Pack
ISBN 978-1-009-23180-0 Student's Book with Digital Pack A
ISBN 978-1-009-23181-7 Student's Book with Digital Pack B
ISBN 978-1-108-40898-1 Workbook with Audio
ISBN 978-1-108-40863-9 Workbook with Audio A
ISBN 978-1-108-41192-9 Workbook with Audio B
ISBN 978-1-108-40516-4 Teacher's Edition with Test Generator
ISBN 978-1-108-41065-6 Presentation Plus
ISBN 978-1-108-41202-5 Class Audio CDs
ISBN 978-1-108-40788-5 Video Resource Book with DVD
ISBN 978-1-009-23152-7 Full Contact with Digital Pack

Additional resources for this publication at www.cambridge.org/evolve

ACKNOWLEDGMENTS

The *Evolve* publishers would like to thank the following individuals and institutions who have contributed their time and insights into the development of the course:

José A. Alvarado Sotelo, **Summit English**, Mexico; Maria Araceli Hernández Tovar, **Instituto Tecnológico Superior de San Luis Potosí**, Capital, Mexico; Rosario Aste Rentería, **Instituto De Emprendedores USIL**, Peru; Kayla M. Briggs, **Hoseo University**, South Korea; Lenise Butler, **Laureate**, Mexico; Lílian Dantas; Aslı Derin Anaç, **İstanbul Bilgi University**, Turkey; Devon Derksen, **Myongji University**, South Korea; Roberta Freitas, **IBEU**, Rio de Janeiro, Brazil; Monica Frenzel, **Universidad Andrés Bello**, Chile; Gloria González Meza, **Instituto Politecnico Nacional, ESCA (University)**, Mexico; Elsa de loa Angeles Hernández Chérrez, **Centro de Idiomas, Universidad Técnica de Ambato**, Ecuador; José Manuel Cuin Jacuinde, **Coordinación de Lenguas Extranjeras del Instituto Tecnológico de Morelia**, Mexico; Thomas Christian Keller, **Universidad de las Américas**, Chile; Daniel Lowe, **Lowe English Services**, Panama; Antonio Machuca Montalvo, **Organización The Institute TITUELS, Veracruz**, Mexico; Daniel Martin, **CELLEP**, Brazil; Ivanova Monteros, **Universidad Tecnológica Equinoccial**, Ecuador; Verónica Nolivos Arellano, Language Coordinator, Quito, Ecuador; Daniel Nowatnick, **USA**; Claudia Piccoli Díaz, **Harmon Hall**, Mexico; Diego Ribeiro Santos, **Universidade Anhembi Morumbi**, São Paulo, Brazil; Maria del Socorro, **Universidad Autonoma del Estado de Mexico, Centro de enseñanza de lenguas (Toluca)**, Mexico; Heidi Vande Voort Nam, **Chongshin University**, South Korea; Isabela Villas Boas, **Casa Thomas Jefferson**, Brasilia, Brazil; Jason Williams, **Notre Dame Seishin University**, Japan; Matthew Wilson, **Miyagi University**, Japan.

To our student contributors, who have given us their ideas and their time, and who appear throughout this book:

Alessandra Avelar, Brazil; Noemi Irene Contreras Yañez, Mexico; Celeste María Erazo Flores, Honduras; Caio Henrique Gogenhan, Brazil; Lorena Martos Ahijado, Spain; Allison Raquel, Peru; Seung Geyoung Yang, South Korea.

And special thanks to Katy Simpson, teacher and writer at *myenglishvoice.com*; and Raquel Ribeiro dos Santos, EFL teacher, EdTech researcher, blogger, and lecturer.

Authors' Acknowledgments:

The authors would like to thank Daniel Isern for all his support in the early stages of the project. This book is dedicated to Groc.

The authors and publishers acknowledge the following sources of copyright material and are grateful for the permissions granted. While every effort has been made, it has not always been possible to identify the sources of all the material used, or to trace all copyright holders. If any omissions are brought to our notice, we will be happy to include the appropriate acknowledgements on reprinting and in the next update to the digital edition, as applicable.

Text:

Charles P. Gerba for the text on p. 98 from 'Hidden dangers in your office' by Dan Townend, *Express Newspapers* website, 12.06.2007. Copyright © Charles P. Gerba. Reproduced with kind permission; The Atlantic Media Co. for the text on p. 104 from 'A Musician Afraid of Sound' by Janet Horvath, 20.10.2015. Copyright © 2015 The Atlantic Media Co., as first published in the *Atlantic Magazine*. All rights reserved. Distributed by Tribune Content Agency.

Photos:

Key: B = Below, BG = Background, BL = Below Left, BR = Below Right, C = Centre, CL = Centre Left, CR = Centre Right, L = Left, R = Right, T = Top, TC = Top Centre, TL = Top Left, TR = Top Right.

All images are sourced from Getty Images.

p. xvi (photo 1): Klaus Vedfelt/DigitalVision; p. xvi (photo 2): Cultura RM Exclusive/dotdotred; p. 1: Artur Debat/Moment; p. 2 (Cecilia): Juanmonino/iStock/Getty Images Plus; p. 2 (students), p. 94 (woman jewelry): PeopleImages/DigitalVision; p. 2 (Marta): Imanol Lpez/EyeEm; p. 2 (siblings): Michael Prince/Corbis; p. 2 (crowd): John Lund/Blend Images; p. 2 (Marcos): Anthony Charles/Cultura; p. 6 (BL): shapecharge/E+; p. 6 (BR): PeopleImages/E+; p. 7: pixelfit/E+; p. 9, p. 18 (photo a), p. 29 (B), p. 62 (photo c), p. 94 (advt baby): Bloomberg; p. 10, 20, 30, 42, 52, 62, 74, 84, 94, 106, 116, 126: Tom Merton/Caiaimage; p. 10 (twins): James Woodson/Photodisc; p. 10 (costumes): John Lund/Sam Diephuis/Blend Images; p .10 (graduates): kali9/E+; p. 10 (cooking): Scott T. Smith/Corbis Documentary; p. 11: Geber86/E+; p. 12: T3 Magazine/Future; p. 13: LucaZola/Photographer's Choice; p. 14 (calendar): Iserg/iStock/Getty Images Plus; p. 14 (document): lumpynoodles/DigitalVision Vectors; p. 14 (headphones): deepblue4you/iStock/Getty Images Plus; p. 14 (keyboard): einegraphic/iStock/Getty Images Plus; p. 14 (mouse): jjltd/DigitalVision Vectors; p. 14 (notepad notes): ctermit/iStock/Getty Images Plus; p. 14 (electrical outlet): kostsov/iStock/Getty Images Plus; p. 14 (screen): tovovan/iStock/Getty Images Plus; p. 14 (spine): Irina Kit/iStock/Getty Images Plus; p. 14 (wifi): Amin Yusifov/iStock/Getty Images Plus; p. 14 (park): Maremagnum/Photolibrary; p. 14 (coffee shop): monkeybusinessimages/iStock/Getty Images Plus; p. 14 (suburban train): VCG/Visual China Group; p. 16, p. 57, p. 86 (necklace): Jose Luis Pelaez Inc/Blend Images/Getty Images Plus; p. 17, p. 68 (drinking coffee), p. 121: Westend61; p. 18 (photo b): Ron Dahlquist/Perspectives; p. 18 (photo c): Endre Majoros/EyeEm; p. 18 (photo d): Sharon Mccutcheon/EyeEm; p. 18 (photo e): Oli Scarff/Getty Images News; p. 19 (photo a): RedlineVector/iStock/Getty Images Plus; p. 19 (photo b): RaStudio/iStock/Getty Images Plus; p. 19 (photo c): LCOSMO/iStock/Getty Images Plus; p. 19 (person standing): gece33/E+; p. 20 (teenager): XiXinXing/iStock/Getty Images Plus; p. 20 (female 20s): Dimitri Otis/Taxi; p. 20 (aged female),(male 20s), p.30 (tennis), p. 90 (TR), p. 96: Hero Images; p. 21: Paul Gilham/Getty Images Sport; p. 22 (team): sampics/Corbis Sport; p. 22 (fans): AfricaImages/iStock/Getty Images Plus; p. 22 (score), p. 69 (food truck): Wavebreakmedia/iStock/Getty Images Plus; p. 22 (tennis court): David Madison/Photographer's Choice; p. 22 (soccer field): Arctic-Images/DigitalVision; p. 22 (swimming pool): ewg3D/E+; p. 22 (female athelete): Syldavia/iStock/Getty Images Plus; p. 22 (race): Michael H/Taxi Japan; p. 22 (gym): Matthew Leete/DigitalVision; p. 22 (ball net): AFP; p. 22 (3d ball): evrenselbaris/DigitalVision Vectors; p. 22 (3d tennis): medobear/DigitalVision Vectors; p. 24 (photo a): Buda Mendes/Getty Images Sport; p. 24 (photo b): Julian Finney/Getty Images Sport; p. 24 (photo c): Adam Pretty/Getty Images Sport; p. 26 (TR): Kevork Djansezian/Getty Images News; p. 26 (TL): Portland Press Herald; p. 28 (bike riding), p. 30 (basketball): Thomas Barwick/Taxi; p. 28 (bike station): agcuesta/iStock Editorial/Getty Images Plus; p. 29 (black male), p. 68 (tasting): JGI/Jamie Grill/Blend Images; p. 29 (old male): Marc Romanelli/Blend Images; p. 29 (black female): Plume Creative/DigitalVision; p. 29 (white female): Dougal Waters/DigitalVision; p. 29 (white couple): Giorgio Fochesato/Photographer's Choice; p. 29 (T): konradlew/E+; p. 30 (running track): Yellow Dog Productions/Iconica; p. 30 (swimming pool): Peter Cade/The Image Bank; p. 30 (soccer): FatCamera/E+; p. 30 (park exercise): AlexSava/E+; p. 30 (mobile screen): Jonathan Daniel/Getty Images Sport; p. 32: Steve Debenport/E+; p. 33: PorasChaudhary/Stone; p. 35: Paul Bradbury/Caiaimage; p. 42 (cat): MASAO OTA/amana images; p. 42 (jewellery): Lisa Bennett/EyeEm; p. 42 (jar): kiboka/iStock/Getty Images Plus; p. 42 (candle): Nicklas Karlsson/EyeEm; p. 43, p. 62 (photo a): Hindustan Times; p. 46 (watch): Davies and Starr/The Image Bank; p. 46 (graduates): EMMANUEL DUNAND/AFP; p. 46 (new employee): MILATAS; p. 46 (couple): photosindia; p. 46 (couple baby): Chris Ryan/OJO Images; p. 46 (question mark): Kritchanut/iStock/Getty Images Plus; p. 46 (map): young84/iStock/Getty Images Plus; p. 46 (stethoscope): MicrovOne/iStock/Getty Images Plus; p. 46 (trophy): Magnilion/DigitalVision Vectors; p. 51: ilbusca/E+; p. 52: Keystone/Hulton Archive; p. 54: Neville Elder/Corbis Historical; p. 56 (photo a): Gerard Fritz/Photographer's Choice; p. 56 (photo b): moodboard/Cultura; p. 56 (photo c): Antenna; p. 58 (electric store): jmalov/E+; p. 58 (pharmacy): JackF/iStock/Getty Images Plus; p. 58 (nail clipper): terex/iStock/Getty Images Plus; p. 58 (adaptor): costinc79/iStock/Getty Images Plus; p. 60 (photo b): drnadig/iStock/Getty Images Plus; p. 60 (photo c): Gregor Schuster/Photographer's Choice; p. 62 (photo b): Scott Olson/Getty Images News; p. 62 (photo d): ROLF VENNENBERND/DPA; p. 64: Steve Stringer Photography/Moment; p. 66 (jar): Elizabeth Watt/Photolibrary; p. 66 (burger): LauriPatterson/E+; p. 66 (lettuce): Suzifoo/E+; p. 66 (chilli): Max2611/iStock/Getty Images Plus; p. 66 (strawberry): Samuel Jimenez/EyeEm; p. 66 (cereal): David Marsden/Photolibrary; p. 66 (yoghurt): Photoevent/E+; p. 66 (jam): Andy Crawford; p. 66 (corn): Diana Miller/Cultura; p. 66 (noodles): JTB Photo/ Universal Images Group Editorial; p. 66 (pasta): SvetlanaK/iStock/Getty Images Plus; p. 66 (salmon): Science Photo Library; p. 66 (avocado): Creative Crop/Photodisc; p. 66 (salt mill): Maximilian Stock Ltd./Photolibrary; p. 68 (egg): RyersonClark/iStock/Getty Images Plus; p. 68 (roast): StockFood; p. 68 (fish): yuriz/iStock/Getty Images Plus; p. 68 (raw): ShyMan/E+; p. 68 (vegetables): Cristian Bortes/EyeEm; p. 68 (chilli): DianePeacock/E+; p. 68 (burgers grill): AVNphotolab/iStock/Getty Images Plus; p. 68 (eating lemon): Daniel Day/The Image Bank; p. 69 (que): Tetra Images; p. 70: BROOK PIFER/Taxi; p. 71: Eerik/E+; p. 73: Monty Rakusen/Cultura; p. 74 (meat): Jupiterimages/Stockbyte; p. 74 (cakes): DragonImages/iStock/Getty Images Plus; p. 74 (salad): fcafotodigital/iStock/Getty Images Plus; p. 75: Andrew Holt/The Image Bank; p. 76 (Deborah): Peathegee Inc/Blend Images; p. 76 (nico): heres2now.com/Moment; p. 76 (apartment): janeff/iStock/Getty Images Plus; p. 77 (opera house): Danita Delimont/Gallo Images; p. 77 (sugarloaf): Eduardo Garcia/Photographer's Choice; p. 77 (Golden Bridge): Jhoanna Reyes/EyeEm; p. 77 (Colisseum): Michael Duva/The Image Bank; p. 77 (Independence Monument): Jeremy Woodhouse/Photodisc; p. 77 (Mt. Fuji): I love Photo and Apple./Moment; p. 80: andresr/E+; p. 81: Roberto Machado Noa/LightRocket; p. 82 (man airport): Dana Neely/The Image Bank; p. 82 (woman airport): Hinterhaus Productions/Taxi; p. 83: kiszon pascal/Moment; p. 84 (theme park): Lou Jones/Lonely Planet Images; p. 84 (market): Linka A Odom/Taxi; p. 84 (event): GDT/ The Image Bank; p. 85: DreamPictures/Vstock/Blend Images; p. 86 (boys tie): Steve Hix/Corbis; p. 86 (stylish): KristinaJovanovic/iStock/Getty Images Plus; p. 86 (socks): Laura Doss/Corbis/Getty Images Plus; p. 86 (bracelet): John Warburton-Lee/AWL Images; p. 86 (formals): Dave and Les Jacobs/Blend Images; p. 86 (20s man): Compassionate Eye Foundation/Hero Images/Taxi; p. 87: PeopleImages/E+; p. 88: Mark Hall/The Image Bank; p. 89: Jonathan Oswaldo Enriquez Huerta/EyeEm; p. 90 (TL): Nick David/Taxi; p. 91 (shirts): Gusto Images/Photodisc; p. 91 (shoes): Jan Stromme/The Image Bank; p. 91 (sunglasses): Koukichi Takahashi/EyeEm; p. 92 (photo a): UberImages/iStock/Getty Images Plus; p. 92 (photo b): Car Culture/Car Culture ® Collection; p. 92 (photo c): Christian Nittinger/EyeEm; p. 92 (photo d): Monashee Frantz/OJO Images; p. 94 (woman headphones): valentinrussanov/E+; p. 97: Harith Samarawickrama/Moment Open; p. 98 (chef): Jose Luis Pelaez Inc/ Blend Images; p. 98 (therapist): BSIP/Universal Images Group; p. 98 (mechanic): Jamie Garbutt/The Image Bank; p. 98 (architect): Letizia Le Fur/ONOKY; p. 98 (paramedic): LPETTET/E+; p. 98 (lawyer): RichLegg/E+; p. 98 (bacteria): Science Stills/Visuals Unlimited, Inc./Visuals Unlimited; p. 99: Stephanie Maze/Corbis Documentary; p. 101: Bill Varie/Corbis; p. 102: Brian Pieters/The Image Bank; p. 103 (band aid): wabeno/iStock/Getty Images Pluswabeno; p. 103 (plaster): Peter Dazeley/Photographer's Choice and Daniel Sambraus/EyeEm; p. 103 (blue plaster): Ccaetano/iStock/Getty Images Plus; p. 104: sot/Taxi; p. 106 (cops): LukaTDB/ iStock/Getty Images Plus; p. 106 (cooking): Jon Feingersh/Blend Images; p. 106 (renovation): GeorgePeters/iStock/Getty Images Plus; p. 106 (backpacker): Auscape/Universal Images Group; p. 107: milos-kreckovic/iStock/Getty Images Plus; p. 108 (Elena): Antonio_Diaz/iStock/Getty Images Plus; p. 108 (Maria): Blend Images - Frida Marquez/Brand X Pictures; p. 109: Anadolu Agency; p. 110 (male): michaelpuche/iStock/Getty Images Plus; p. 110 (young female): Sandeep Kapoor/EyeEm; p. 110 (old female): Shannon Fagan/Taxi; p. 111: AntonioGuillem/iStock/Getty Images Plus; p. 112 (broken phone): Ariel Skelley/DigitalVision; p. 112 (selfie): Betsie Van Der Meer/Taxi; p. 113: martinedoucet/E+; p. 116 (girl): JohnnyGreig/E+; p. 116 (food): mediaphotos/E+; p. 116 (tutorial): fstop123/E+; p. 117: Mint Images - Frans Lanting/Mint Images; p. 118 (wet): Tim Robberts/ Taxi; p. 118 (cold): Attila Kocsis/EyeEm; p. 118 (hot): Karwai Tang/WireImage; p. 118 (stormy): john finney photography/Moment; p. 118 (extreme): Scott B Smith Photography/Photolibrary; p. 119: Christopher Wirth/EyeEm; p. 120 (quito): Reinier Snijders/EyeEm; p. 120 (tortoise): Antonio Salinas L./Moment; p. 122 (mobile): Bill Diodato/Corbis Documentary; p. 122 (nature): John Turp/Moment; p. 123 (Jason Hawkes/The Image Bank); p. 124 (gardening): Beau Lark/Corbis/VCG; p. 124 (flower): Laizah Mae Tano/EyeEm; p. 125: Kory Rogers/EyeEm; p. 126 (beach): Jeremy Koreski/All Canada Photos; p. 126 (lake): Aimin Tang/Photographer's Choice; p. 126 (rockies): TerenceLeezy/Moment; p. 141 (bottle): thumb/iStock/Getty Images Plus; p. 141 (cream): Anthony Lee/Caiaimage; p. 141 (umbrella): kaisphoto/E+; p. 141 (candy bar): Chee Siong Teh/EyeEm; p. 141 (tissue): Mimadeo/iStock/Getty Images Plus; p. 149 (black man): verity jane smith/Blend Images; p. 149 (white girl): T. Fuchs/F1online; p. 149 (feet): baona/iStock/Getty Images Plus; p. 152 (photo a): fralo/iStock/Getty Images Plus; p. 152 (photo b): Gillian Henry/Moment; p. 152 (photo c): sara_winter/iStock/Getty Images Plus; p. 152 (photo d): Image Source/DigitalVision; p. 152 (photo e): Sam's photography/Moment; p. 157 (photo a): Coprid/iStock/Getty Images Plus; p. 157 (photo b): homeworks255/iStock/Getty Images Plus; p. 157 (photo c): LotusWorks/iStock/Getty Images Plus; p. 157 (photo d): bergamont/iStock/Getty Images Plus; p. 157 (photo e): mbtaichi/iStock/Getty Images Plus; p. 160 (photo a): ballyscanlon/Stockbyte; p. 160 (photo b): PC Plus Magazine/Future; p. 160 (photo c): elfinima/E+; p. 160 (photo d): AlexLMX/iStock/Getty Images Plus; p. 160 (photo e): Viktorus/iStock/Getty Images Plus.

The following images are sourced from other sources:

p. 18 (The 7 Habits of Highly Effective People): Courtesy of Franklin Covey Co; p. 72 (Impossible Burger): Courtesy of Impossible Foods Inc.

Clipart Courtesy of Noun Project Inc.

Front cover photography by Alija/E+/Getty Images.

Illustrations by: 290 Sean (KJA Artists) pp. 4, 5, 100; Denis Cristo (Sylvie Poggio Artists Agency) pp. 12, 78; Ana Djordjevic (Astound US) pp. 20, 88; Lyn Dylan (Sylvie Poggio Artists Agency) pp. 2, 76; Joanna Kerr (New Division) p. 15; Dusan Lakicevic (Beehive illustration) pp. 15, 25; Martin Sanders (Beehive illustration) pp. 120, 152; Mark Watkinson (Illustration Web) p. 67; Liav Zabari (Lemonade illustration) p. 23.

Audio production by CityVox, New York

EVOLVE

SPEAKING MATTERS

EVOLVE is a six-level American English course for adults and young adults, taking students from beginner to advanced levels (CEFR A1 to C1).

Drawing on insights from language teaching experts and real students, EVOLVE is a general English course that gets students speaking with confidence.

This student-centered course covers all skills and focuses on the most effective and efficient ways to make progress in English.

Confidence in teaching.
Joy in learning.

Better Learning WITH EVOLVE

Better Learning is our simple approach where insights we've gained from research have helped shape content that drives results. Language evolves, and so does the way we learn. This course takes a flexible, student-centered approach to English language teaching.

Meet our student contributors

Videos and ideas from real students feature throughout the Student's Book.

Our student contributors describe themselves in three words.

ALESSANDRA AVELAR
Creative, positive, funny
Faculdade ICESP, Águas Claras, Brazil

NOEMI IRENE CONTRERAS YAÑEZ
Funny, intelligent, optimistic
Universidad del Valle de México, Mexico

CELESTE MARÍA ERAZO FLORES
Happy, special, friendly
Unitec (Universidad Tecnologica Centroamericana), Honduras

CAIO HENRIQUE GOGENHAN
Funny, lovely, smart
Universidade Anhembi Morumbi, Brazil

ALLISON RAQUEL
Friendly, cheerful, intelligent
Universidad Privada del Norte, Peru

SEUNG GEYOUNG YANG
Happy, creative
Myongji University, South Korea

LORENA MARTOS AHIJADO
Cheerful, positive, kind
Universidad Europea de Madrid, Spain

Student-generated content

EVOLVE is the first course of its kind to feature real student-generated content. We spoke to over 2,000 students from all over the world about the topics they would like to discuss in English and in what situations they would like to be able to speak more confidently.

The ideas are included throughout the Student's Book and the students appear in short videos responding to discussion questions.

INSIGHT

Research shows that achievable speaking role models can be a powerful motivator.

CONTENT

Bite-sized videos feature students talking about topics in the Student's Book.

RESULT

Students are motivated to speak and share their ideas.

"It's important to provide learners with interesting or stimulating topics."

Teacher, Mexico (Global Teacher Survey, 2017)

Find it

INSIGHT

Research with hundreds of teachers and students across the globe revealed a desire to expand the classroom and bring the real world in.

CONTENT

Find it are smartphone activities that allow students to bring live content into the class and personalize the learning experience with research and group activities.

RESULT

Students engage in the lesson because it is meaningful to them.

Designed for success

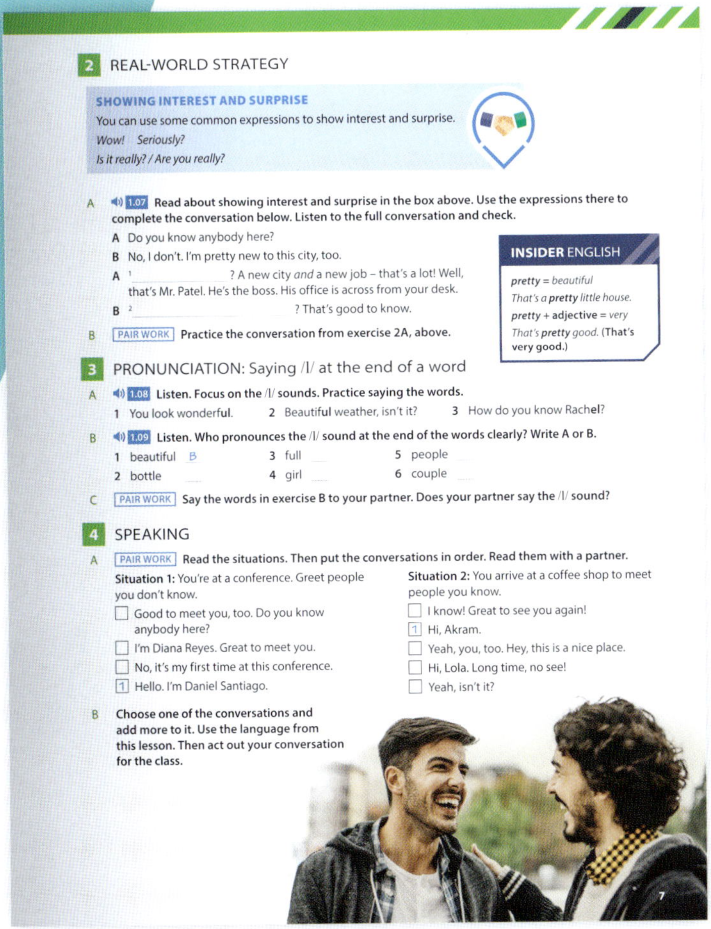
2 REAL-WORLD STRATEGY

SHOWING INTEREST AND SURPRISE

You can use some common expressions to show interest and surprise.

Wow! *Seriously?*

Is it really? / Are you really?

A 1.07 **Read about showing interest and surprise in the box above. Use the expressions there to complete the conversation below. Listen to the full conversation and check.**

A Do you know anybody here?

B No, I don't. I'm pretty new to this city, too.

A [1] ______________ ? A new city *and* a new job – that's a lot! Well, that's Mr. Patel. He's the boss. His office is across from your desk.

B [2] ______________ ? That's good to know.

B PAIR WORK **Practice the conversation from exercise 2A, above.**

INSIDER ENGLISH

pretty = *beautiful*

*That's a **pretty** little house.*

***pretty* + adjective** = *very*

*That's **pretty** good.* **(That's very good.)**

3 PRONUNCIATION: Saying /l/ at the end of a word

A 1.08 **Listen. Focus on the /l/ sounds. Practice saying the words.**

1 You look wonderful. 2 Beautiful weather, isn't it? 3 How do you know Rachel?

B 1.09 **Listen. Who pronounces the /l/ sound at the end of the words clearly? Write A or B.**

1 beautiful B 3 full ___ 5 people ___

2 bottle ___ 4 girl ___ 6 couple ___

C PAIR WORK **Say the words in exercise B to your partner. Does your partner say the /l/ sound?**

4 SPEAKING

A PAIR WORK **Read the situations. Then put the conversations in order. Read them with a partner.**

Situation 1: You're at a conference. Greet people you don't know.

- ☐ Good to meet you, too. Do you know anybody here?
- ☐ I'm Diana Reyes. Great to meet you.
- ☐ No, it's my first time at this conference.
- 1 Hello. I'm Daniel Santiago.

Situation 2: You arrive at a coffee shop to meet people you know.

- ☐ I know! Great to see you again!
- 1 Hi, Akram.
- ☐ Yeah, you, too. Hey, this is a nice place.
- ☐ Hi, Lola. Long time, no see!
- ☐ Yeah, isn't it?

B **Choose one of the conversations and add more to it. Use the language from this lesson. Then act out your conversation for the class.**

7

Pronunciation

INSIGHT

Research shows that only certain aspects of pronunciation actually affect comprehensibility and inhibit communication.

CONTENT

EVOLVE focuses on the aspects of pronunciation that most affect communication.

RESULT

Students understand more when listening and can be clearly understood when they speak.

Insider English

INSIGHT

Even in a short exchange, idiomatic language can inhibit understanding.

CONTENT

Insider English focuses on the informal language and colloquial expressions frequently found in everyday situations.

RESULT

Students are confident in the real world.

1.1 WE'RE FAMILY

LESSON OBJECTIVE
- talk about the people in your life

1 VOCABULARY: Describing people you know

A 1.03 Look at the pictures. Listen and say the words. Who do you see every day?

1 neighbors 2 classmates 3 close friends 4 couple girlfriend boyfriend 5 boss 6 grandchildren grandson granddaughter 7 roommates

B Now do the vocabulary exercises for 1.1 on page 141.

C PAIR WORK Make five true sentences with five words from exercise 1A. Tell your partner.

2 LANGUAGE IN CONTEXT

A Look at the picture of Cecilia. Who are the people in her life? Who's in her family? Check (✓) the boxes.

These are my classmates. That's Kiko and Luis on the left. They're from different countries, but we all study English.

Here are my brother and sister. Their names are Jose Luis and Yvonne. This is an old photo.

I have more than 200 friends on Facebook, but they're not close friends. Many people are coworkers or school friends.

This is Marta. We're close friends. She's a student in Puebla.

My name's Cecilia, and I'm from Puebla, in Mexico. I'm an English student now, in Bakersfield, California. These are the people in my life.

People always ask, "Is he your boyfriend?" No, he's not! He's my neighbor, Marcos, and he's a friend.

B Match the names with their connection to Cecilia.

1 Yvonne a neighbor
2 Marta b close friend
3 Kiko and Luis c sister
4 Jose Luis d classmates
5 Marcos e brother

2

3 GRAMMAR: be; possessive adjectives

A Complete the rules below. Use the sentences in the grammar box to help you.
1 I'm from Puebla. I'm = I am
2 They're not close friends. You can also say: They close friends.
3 Is he your boyfriend? To answer, you can say: Yes, he is. or No, he .

be		
I'm from Puebla.	I'm not from Bakersfield.	Am I late?
She's a student in Puebla.	He's not my boyfriend.	Is he your classmate?
We're close friends.	They're not close friends.	Are you my new neighbor?

B Complete the spaces with the correct possessive adjective. Use the sentences in the grammar box to help you.
I my , you , he , she , it . we , they .

Possessive adjectives		
He's my brother.	His name's Jose Luis.	They are our neighbors.
What's your name?	Her name's Marta.	He is their son.
	The dog hurt its foot.	

C Now go to page 129. Look at the grammar chart and do the grammar exercise for 2.1.

D GROUP WORK Use the words to write questions. Then read the Accuracy check box and check your work. Use the questions to find out more about your classmates.
1 his / what's / name / ? What's his name?
2 from / is / where / she / ?
3 is / name / her / Maria / ?
4 they / from / are / Argentina / ?
5 our / is / teacher / American / ?
6 are / from / where / parents / your / ?

ACCURACY CHECK
Possessive adjectives agree with the possessor.
This is a photo of my wife with ~~their~~ parents. ✗
This is a photo of my wife with her parents. ✓

4 SPEAKING

A Look at the picture of Cecilia and her connections on page 2. Make a similar picture for your life. Write the names of your connections. Watch Seung Geyoung's video.

REAL STUDENT
What family members does she say? Are they the same as your family?

B PAIR WORK Ask and answer questions about your pictures. You can show photos of the people on your phone.

Who is Rogelio? He's a coworker at my office.
Are Bob and Vera your parents? Yes, they are.

3

ACCURACY CHECK

Possessive adjectives agree with the possessor.

This is a photo of my wife with ~~their~~ parents. ✗

This is a photo of my wife with her parents. ✓

Accuracy check

INSIGHT

Some common errors can become fossilized if not addressed early on in the learning process.

CONTENT

Accuracy check highlights common learner errors (based on unique research into the Cambridge Learner Corpus) and can be used for self-editing.

RESULT

Students avoid common errors in their written and spoken English.

"The presentation is very clear and there are plenty of opportunities for student practice and production."

Jason Williams, Teacher, Notre Dame Seishin University, Japan

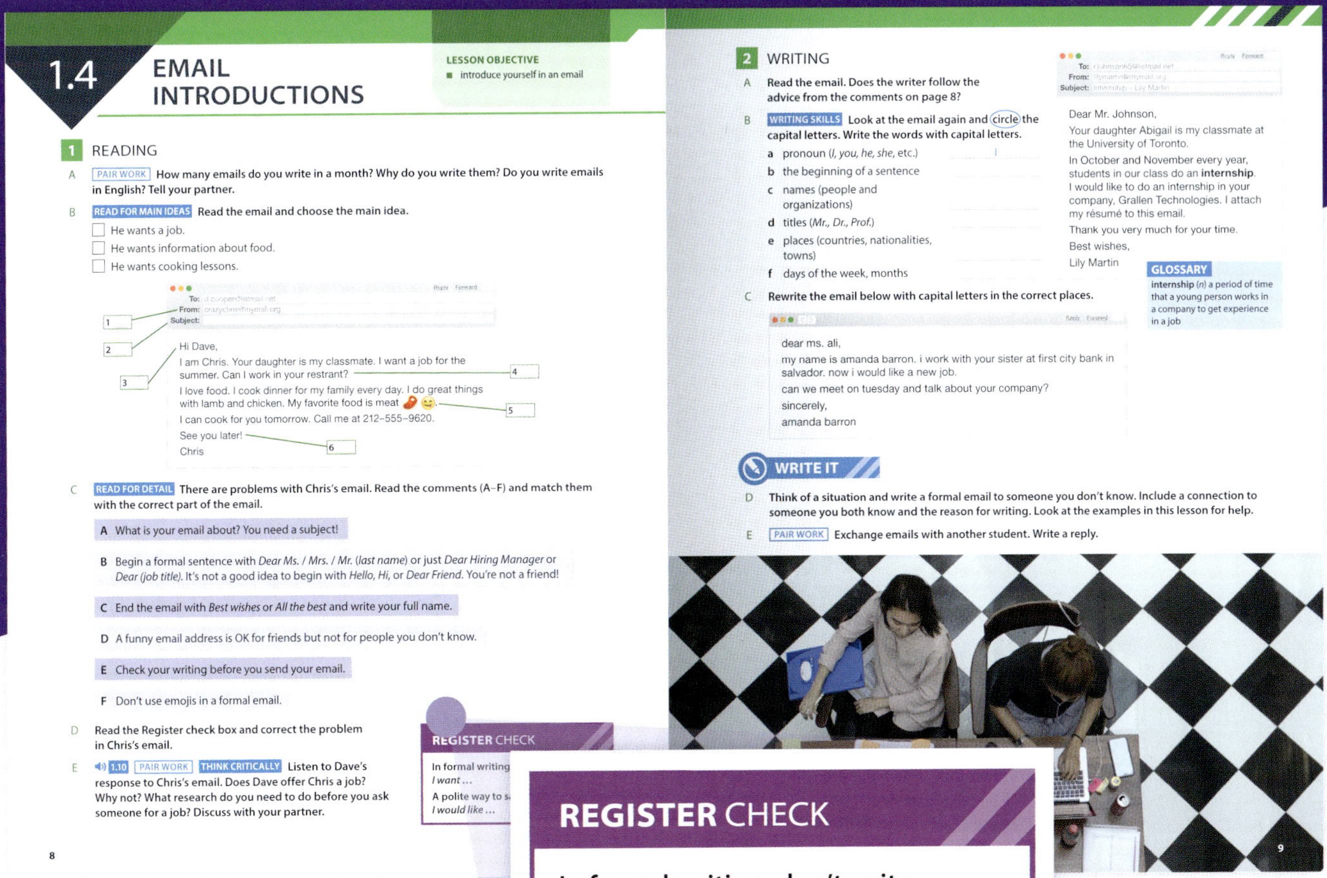

1.4 EMAIL INTRODUCTIONS

LESSON OBJECTIVE
- introduce yourself in an email

1 READING

A PAIR WORK How many emails do you write in a month? Why do you write them? Do you write emails in English? Tell your partner.

B READ FOR MAIN IDEAS Read the email and choose the main idea.

- [ ] He wants a job.
- [ ] He wants information about food.
- [ ] He wants cooking lessons.

To:
From:
Subject:

Hi Dave,

I am Chris. Your daughter is my classmate. I want a job for the summer. Can I work in your restrant?

I love food. I cook dinner for my family every day. I do great things with lamb and chicken. My favorite food is meat.

I can cook for you tomorrow. Call me at 212-555-9620.

See you later!

Chris

1 ___ 2 ___ 3 ___ 4 ___ 5 ___ 6 ___

C READ FOR DETAIL There are problems with Chris's email. Read the comments (A–F) and match them with the correct part of the email.

A What is your email about? You need a subject!

B Begin a formal sentence with *Dear Ms. / Mrs. / Mr. (last name)* or just *Dear Hiring Manager* or *Dear (job title)*. It's not a good idea to begin with *Hello, Hi,* or *Dear Friend*. You're not a friend!

C End the email with *Best wishes* or *All the best* and write your full name.

D A funny email address is OK for friends but not for people you don't know.

E Check your writing before you send your email.

F Don't use emojis in a formal email.

D Read the Register check box and correct the problem in Chris's email.

E 1.10 PAIR WORK THINK CRITICALLY Listen to Dave's response to Chris's email. Does Dave offer Chris a job? Why not? What research do you need to do before you ask someone for a job? Discuss with your partner.

8

2 WRITING

A Read the email. Does the writer follow the advice from the comments on page 8?

B WRITING SKILLS Look at the email again and circle the capital letters. Write the words with capital letters.

a pronoun (*I, you, he, she*, etc.) ___
b the beginning of a sentence ___
c names (people and organizations) ___
d titles (*Mr., Dr., Prof.*) ___
e places (countries, nationalities, towns) ___
f days of the week, months ___

To:
From:
Subject:

Dear Mr. Johnson,

Your daughter Abigail is my classmate at the University of Toronto.

In October and November every year, students in our class do an **internship**. I would like to do an internship in your company, Grallen Technologies. I attach my résumé to this email.

Thank you very much for your time.

Best wishes,

Lily Martin

GLOSSARY
internship (*n*) a period of time that a young person works in a company to get experience in a job

C Rewrite the email below with capital letters in the correct places.

dear ms. ali,

my name is amanda barron. i work with your sister at first city bank in salvador. now i would like a new job.

can we meet on tuesday and talk about your company?

sincerely,

amanda barron

WRITE IT

D Think of a situation and write a formal email to someone you don't know. Include a connection to someone you both know and the reason for writing. Look at the examples in this lesson for help.

E PAIR WORK Exchange emails with another student. Write a reply.

9

REGISTER CHECK

In formal writing, don't write *I want …*

A polite way to say what you want is *I would like …*

Register check

INSIGHT

Teachers report that their students often struggle to master the differences between written and spoken English.

CONTENT

Register check draws on research into the Cambridge English Corpus and highlights potential problem areas for learners.

RESULT

Students transition confidently between written and spoken English and recognize different levels of formality as well as when to use them appropriately.

You spoke. We listened.

Students told us that speaking is the most important skill for them to master, while teachers told us that finding speaking activities which engage their students and work in the classroom can be challenging.

That's why EVOLVE has a whole lesson dedicated to speaking: Lesson 5, *Time to speak*.

Time to speak

INSIGHT

Speaking ability is how students most commonly measure their own progress, but is also the area where they feel most insecure. To be able to fully exploit speaking opportunities in the classroom, students need a safe speaking environment where they can feel confident, supported, and able to experiment with language.

CONTENT

Time to Speak is a unique lesson dedicated to developing speaking skills and is based around immersive tasks which involve information sharing and decision making.

RESULT

Time to speak lessons create a buzz in the classroom where speaking can really thrive, evolve, and take off, resulting in more confident speakers of English.

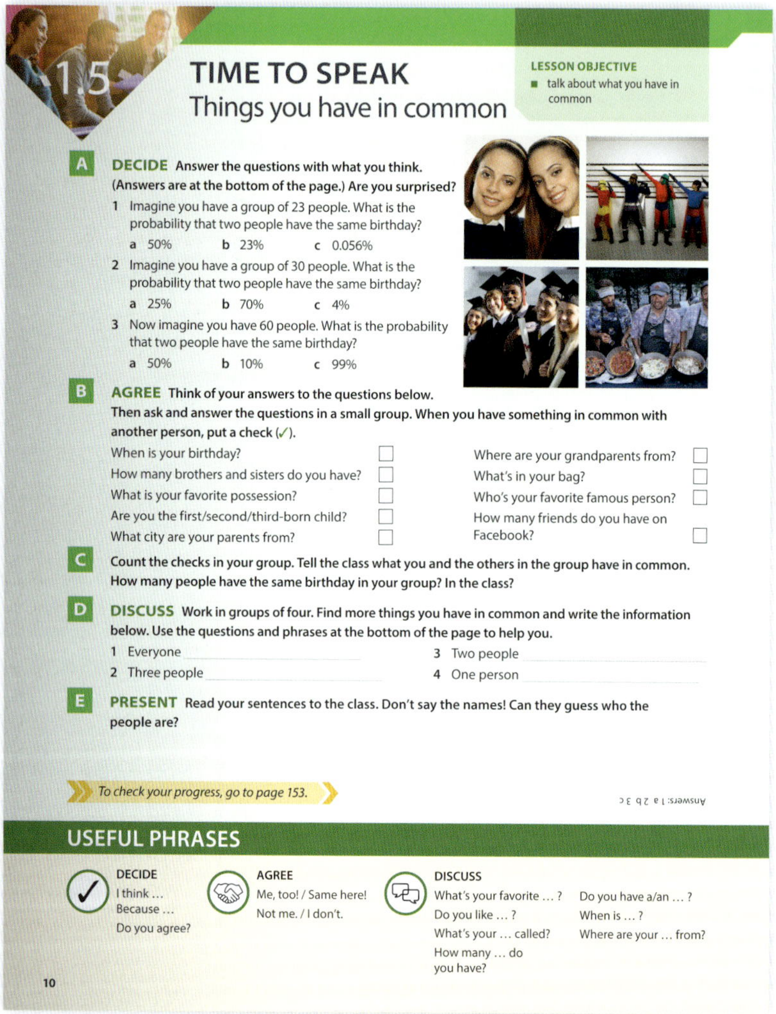

1.5 TIME TO SPEAK
Things you have in common

LESSON OBJECTIVE
- talk about what you have in common

A DECIDE Answer the questions with what you think. (Answers are at the bottom of the page.) Are you surprised?

1 Imagine you have a group of 23 people. What is the probability that two people have the same birthday?
a 50% b 23% c 0.056%

2 Imagine you have a group of 30 people. What is the probability that two people have the same birthday?
a 25% b 70% c 4%

3 Now imagine you have 60 people. What is the probability that two people have the same birthday?
a 50% b 10% c 99%

B AGREE Think of your answers to the questions below. Then ask and answer the questions in a small group. When you have something in common with another person, put a check (✓).

When is your birthday? ☐
How many brothers and sisters do you have? ☐
What is your favorite possession? ☐
Are you the first/second/third-born child? ☐
What city are your parents from? ☐
Where are your grandparents from? ☐
What's in your bag? ☐
Who's your favorite famous person? ☐
How many friends do you have on Facebook? ☐

C Count the checks in your group. Tell the class what you and the others in the group have in common. How many people have the same birthday in your group? In the class?

D DISCUSS Work in groups of four. Find more things you have in common and write the information below. Use the questions and phrases at the bottom of the page to help you.

1 Everyone ______
2 Three people ______
3 Two people ______
4 One person ______

E PRESENT Read your sentences to the class. Don't say the names! Can they guess who the people are?

To check your progress, go to page 153.

Answers: 1 a 2 b 3 c

USEFUL PHRASES

DECIDE
I think …
Because …
Do you agree?

AGREE
Me, too! / Same here!
Not me. / I don't.

DISCUSS
What's your favorite … ?
Do you like … ?
What's your … called?
How many … do you have?
Do you have a/an … ?
When is … ?
Where are your … from?

10

Experience Better Learning with EVOLVE: a course that helps both teachers and students on every step of the language learning journey.

Speaking matters. Find out more about creating safe speaking environments in the classroom.

EVOLVE unit structure

Unit opening page

Each unit opening page activates prior knowledge and vocabulary and immediately gets students speaking.

Lessons 1 and 2

These lessons present and practice the unit vocabulary and grammar in context, helping students discover language rules for themselves. Students then have the opportunity to use this language in well-scaffolded, personalized speaking tasks.

Lesson 3

This lesson is built around a functional language dialogue that models and contextualizes useful fixed expressions for managing a particular situation. This is a real world strategy to help students handle unexpected conversational turns.

Lesson 4

This is a combined skills lesson based around an engaging reading or listening text. Each lesson asks students to think critically and ends with a practical writing task.

Lesson 5

Time to speak is an entire lesson dedicated to developing speaking skills. Students work on collaborative, immersive tasks which involve information sharing and decision making.

CONTENTS

Functional language	Listening	Reading	Writing	Speaking
■ Greet someone for the first time; greet someone who you know; start conversations **Real-world strategy** ■ Show interest and surprise		**Email introductions** ■ Read and correct an email	**A work email** ■ A formal email to someone you don't know ■ Punctuation: capital letters	■ Talk about people you know ■ Ask and answer questions about people in your life ■ Talk about things you have in your bag ■ Say *hello* and start a conversation **Time to speak** ■ Talk about things in common
■ Explain, check, and solve a technology problem **Real-world strategy** ■ Ask for repetition	**How to be successful** ■ A podcast about what successful people do		**A short post on a website** ■ A comment on a website post ■ Use examples and opinions to add interest	■ Talk about your busy life ■ Talk about what you do every day, etc. ■ Talk about work spaces ■ Talk on the phone/online **Time to speak** ■ Talk about apps for work or study
■ Ask for information **Real-world strategy** ■ Check information	**Bike sharing** ■ A report about cycling in Mexico City		**A short social media message** ■ A message to a bike sharing program ■ *and*, *but*, and *so*	■ Talk about sports that are popular in your country ■ Describe who you see ■ Describe exercise routines ■ Ask for information about a swimming pool **Time to speak** ■ Talk about fitness programs
■ Make and accept invitations; plan where and when to meet **Real-world strategy** ■ Give general excuses	**Waiting for something special** ■ A news report about an unusual event		**An invitation to an event** ■ An event announcement ■ *too*, *also*, and *as well*	■ Talk about celebrations in your country ■ Arrange to meet after English class ■ Choose gifts ■ Invite someone to an event **Time to speak** ■ Talk about gifts for a trip
■ React to good and bad news **Real-world strategy** ■ Check your understanding		**First impressions** ■ Posts about experiences in a new place	**Online comments** ■ A comment on a message board ■ Agree and disagree	■ Talk about a special picture of you as a child ■ Talk about a special day in your life ■ Ask and answer questions about last weekend ■ Respond to good and bad news **Time to speak** ■ Talk about a famous event in the past
■ Explain your language problem; explain the function of the thing you want **Real-world strategy** ■ Ask for words in English	**Money lessons** ■ Stories about money problems		**Top tips to save money** ■ A vlog script with suggestions for saving money ■ Using referencing: *one* and *them*	■ Talk about where you shop ■ Plan a shopping trip ■ Talk about shopping habits ■ Explain what you want **Time to speak** ■ Present a new invention

	Learning objectives	Grammar	Vocabulary	Pronunciation
Unit 7 Eat, drink, be happy	■ Talk about your favorite comfort food ■ Design a food truck ■ Explain what you want in a restaurant ■ Write a comment about an online article ■ Plan a party	■ Quantifiers ■ Verb patterns	■ Naming food ■ Describing food	■ /ʤ/ and /g/ sounds
Unit 8 Trips	■ Discuss what to do in your town ■ Talk about a trip you went on ■ Give advice and make suggestions ■ Write advice on living in another country ■ Plan a short trip	■ *if* and *when* ■ Giving reasons using *to* and *for*	■ Traveling ■ Transportation	■ Long and short vowel sounds ■ Listening for intonation
Unit 9 Looking good	■ Compare stores and what they sell ■ Talk about people in photos ■ Ask for and give opinions ■ Write a paragraph describing a photo ■ Create and present an ad	■ Comparative adjectives ■ Superlative adjectives	■ Accessories ■ Appearance	■ /ɜ/ vowel sound
Review 3 (Review of Units 7–9)				
Unit 10 Risky business	■ Talk about how to avoid danger at work ■ Make predictions about your future ■ Describe a medical problem and ask for help ■ Write an email to your future self ■ Plan a reality TV show	■ *have to* ■ Making predictions	■ Jobs ■ Health problems	■ Final consonant sounds
Unit 11 Me, online	■ Talk about what you've done and what you've never done ■ Talk about what you've done, and when ■ Make and respond to requests ■ Write comments about an infographic ■ Create a video or vlog	■ Present perfect for experience ■ Present perfect and simple past	■ Verb-noun internet phrases ■ Social media verbs	■ Final /m/ and /n/ sounds
Unit 12 Outdoors	■ Talk about the weather ■ Describe places, people, and things ■ Ask for and give directions ■ Write simple instructions ■ Create a tourism campaign for your country	■ *be like* ■ Relative pronouns: *who, which, that*	■ Weather ■ Landscapes and cityscapes	■ /w/ at the beginning of a word ■ Listening for *t* when it sounds like d
Review 4 (Review of Units 10–12)				
Grammar charts and practice, pages 129–140 Vocabulary exercises, pages 141–152				

Functional language	Listening	Reading	Writing	Speaking
■ Order food; take an order; ask questions about food; ask for the check **Real-world strategy** ■ *I mean*		**Foods** ■ An article about the Impossible Burger	**Comments on Impossible Foods** ■ A comment on an article ■ *I (don't) think; If you ask me; For me*	■ Talk about special meals ■ Talk about your favorite comfort food ■ Talk about a food truck ■ Order food from a menu **Time to speak** ■ Talk about the perfect party
■ Give advice and make suggestions; respond to advice and suggestions **Real-world strategy** ■ Echo questions	**Leaving home** ■ A radio show about living in another country		**Listeners' comments** ■ A comment on advice from listeners ■ Phrases to respond to advice	■ Talk about a good vacation ■ Talk about your town ■ Talk about a long trip you took ■ Give advice to a visitor in your town **Time to speak** ■ Talk about planning a trip
■ Ask for an opinion; give a positive opinion; give a negative or neutral opinion **Real-world strategy** ■ *I guess*		**Image is everything** ■ An article about advertising	**Advertising contest** ■ An email submission to a contest ■ Punctuation: periods, capital letters, and commas	■ Talk about appearance ■ Compare clothes stores ■ Talk about your best photos ■ Give your opinion of clothes **Time to speak** ■ Talk about making an ad
■ Offer help; ask for information about the problem; ask someone for help **Real-world strategy** ■ *It's like / It feels like*		**Face your fears** ■ An article about a personal experience	**An email to myself** ■ An email giving advice ■ *anyway, by the way*	■ Talk about things you're afraid of ■ Talk about dangers at work or study ■ Predict future events ■ Explain a medical problem **Time to speak** ■ Talk about reality TV
■ Make requests; respond to requests; ask for permission; refusing **Real-world strategy** ■ Remember words		**Selfies** ■ An infographic	**Positive and negative comments** ■ A short comment on selfies ■ Saying something positive or negative	■ Talk about screens ■ Ask and answer questions about experiences ■ Ask and answer questions about online habits ■ Make requests in specific situations **Time to speak** ■ Talk about online videos
■ Ask for directions; give directions **Real-world strategy** ■ Correct yourself	**Guerrilla gardening** ■ An interview with a guerrilla gardener		**How to …** ■ A list of instructions on how to do something ■ *first, then, next, now, finally*	■ Talk about hot and cold weather ■ Talk about weather in different cities in the world ■ Talk about people, objects, and places ■ Ask for directions, check you understand **Time to speak** ■ Talk about advertising your country

CLASSROOM LANGUAGE

1.02 Asking for help

How do you say that in English?
What does ______________ mean?
How do you spell ______________?
How do you pronounce this word?
Sorry, can you repeat that, please?
Sorry, I don't understand.

Working in pairs and groups

Who wants to start?
Who wants to go first?
Whose turn is it?
It's my turn.
It's your turn.
OK. What do you have for number 1?
Let's compare answers.

UNIT OBJECTIVES

- talk about the people in your life
- talk about possessions
- greet people and start a conversation
- introduce yourself in an email
- talk about what you have in common

CONNECTIONS

1

START SPEAKING

A Look at the picture. What is the connection between the people? What are some different ways people are connected? Read the list and add two more.

family friends work/school ________ ________

FIND IT

B Think about a famous actor in your country: how many connections do you have between you and him/her? You can use your phone to help you.

C Are you a very social person in general? Do you have connections with a lot of different people? For ideas, watch Alessandra's video.

REAL STUDENT

Are you the same as Alessandra?

1.1 WE'RE FAMILY

LESSON OBJECTIVE
- talk about the people in your life

1 VOCABULARY: Describing people you know

A 1.03 **Look at the pictures. Listen and say the words. Who do you see every day?**

B **Now do the vocabulary exercises for 1.1 on page 141.**

C PAIR WORK **Make five true sentences with five words from exercise 1A. Tell your partner.**

2 LANGUAGE IN CONTEXT

A **Look at the picture of Cecilia. Who are the people in her life? Who's in her family? Check (✓) the boxes.**

B **Match the names with their connection to Cecilia.**

1	Yvonne	a	neighbor
2	Marta	b	close friend
3	Kiko and Luis	c	sister
4	Jose Luis	d	classmates
5	Marcos	e	brother

3 GRAMMAR: *be*; possessive adjectives

A **Complete the rules below. Use the sentences in the grammar box to help you.**

1 *I'm from Puebla.* *I'm* = ___I am___

2 *They're not close friends.*
You can also say: *They* ________ *close friends.*

3 ***Is** he your boyfriend?*
To answer, you can say:
Yes, he is. or *No, he* ________.

be

I'm from Puebla.	**I'm not** from Bakersfield.	**Am I** late?
She's a student in Puebla.	**He's not** my boyfriend.	**Is** he your classmate?
We're close friends.	**They're not** close friends.	**Are you** my new neighbor?

B **Complete the spaces with the correct possessive adjective. Use the sentences in the grammar box to help you.**

I ___my___, you ________, he ________, she ________,
it ________.
we ________, they ________.

Possessive adjectives

He's **my** brother.	**His** name's Jose Luis.	They are **our** neighbors.
What's **your** name?	**Her** name's Marta.	He is **their** son.
	The dog hurt **its** foot.	

C **Now go to page 129. Look at the grammar chart and do the grammar exercise for 1.1.**

D GROUP WORK **Use the words to write questions. Then read the Accuracy check box and check your work. Use the questions to find out more about your classmates.**

1 his / what's / name / ? ___What's his name?___
2 from / is / where / she / ? ________
3 is / name / her / Maria / ? ________
4 they / from / are / Argentina / ? ________
5 our / is / teacher / American / ? ________
6 are / from / where / parents / your / ? ________

ACCURACY CHECK

Possessive adjectives agree with the possessor.

This is a photo of my wife with ~~their~~ parents. ✗
This is a photo of my wife with her parents. ✓

4 SPEAKING

A **Look at the picture of Cecilia and her connections on page 2. Make a similar picture for your life. Write the names of your connections. Watch Seung Geyoung's video.**

REAL STUDENT

What family members does she say? Are they the same as your family?

FIND IT

B PAIR WORK **Ask and answer questions about your pictures. You can show photos of the people on your phone.**

Who is Rogelio? — He's a coworker at my office.

Are Bob and Vera your parents? — Yes, they are.

1.2 WHAT'S IN YOUR BAG?

LESSON OBJECTIVE
- talk about possessions

1 VOCABULARY: Naming everyday things

A 1.04 **Look at the pictures. Listen and say the words. Do you have these things in your bag?**

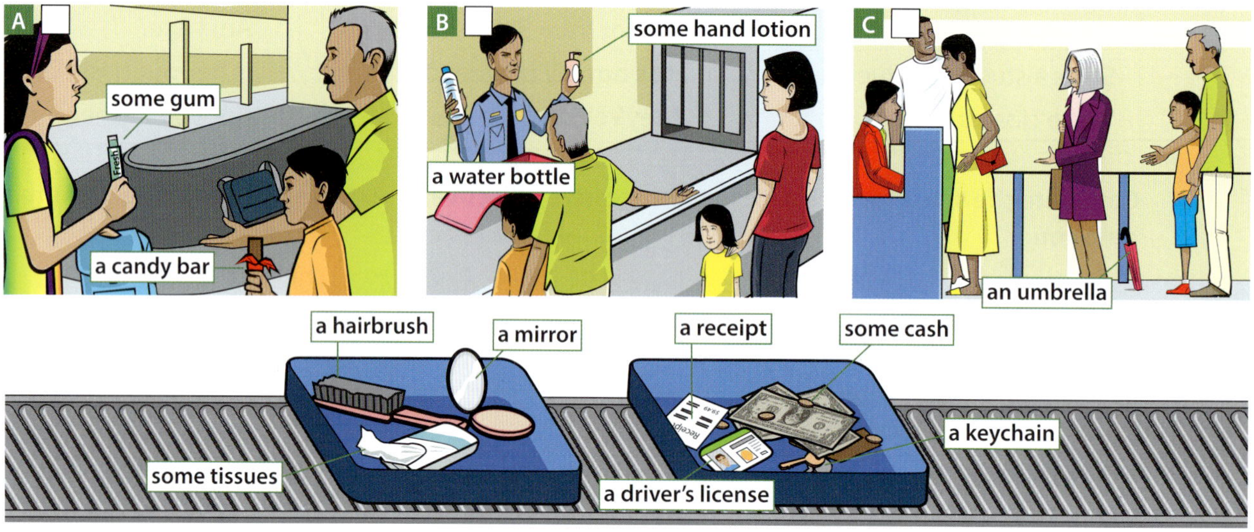

B **Now do the vocabulary exercises for 1.2 on page 141.**

C PAIR WORK **Choose an item from exercise 1A. Your partner asks you questions to guess the item.**

Is it a mirror?
Yes, it is.
Are they tissues?
No, they aren't.

2 LANGUAGE IN CONTEXT

A 1.05 **Look at the pictures in exercise 1A again. Where are the people? Listen to the conversations and match them to the pictures.**

1.05 Audio script

1 A Is that your umbrella?
B No, it's not mine. I think it belongs to those people. Perhaps it's theirs.
A Hmm. Excuse me, is this yours?
C Oh, yes! Thanks. That's my wife's umbrella.
D Thanks so much!

2 A Excuse me! Whose is this?
B It's not ours. I think it's hers – the woman with the little girl there.
A Excuse me, ma'am. Is this yours?
C What? Oh, yes, that's mine.
A I'm sorry, but you can't take hand lotion and a water bottle on the plane.
C But they're my daughter's. She needs them!

3 A I think that's my grandson's bag.
B No, sorry, it isn't his. It's mine. It belongs to me. Look, there's my pack of gum.
A You're right. So where's my grandson's bag?
B There's another blue one. Is that one his?

B 1.05 **Listen again and read. Match the items with their owners.**

1 The water bottle ☐ 2 The umbrella ☐ 3 The blue bag ☐

3 GRAMMAR: Possession

A **Circle the correct answers. Use the sentences in the grammar box to help you.**

1 Which response is <u>not</u> correct: *Whose is this?*

- **a** *It's mine.*
- **b** *It's black.*
- **c** *It's my grandson's bag.*
- **d** *It belongs to me.*

2 What comes after *my*?

- **a** a noun
- **b** nothing

3 What comes after *mine*?

- **a** a noun
- **b** nothing

4 What does the *'s* in *my grandson's bag* mean?

- **a** *is*
- **b** it shows possession

Possession

That's **my** grandson's bag.
No, sorry. It isn't **his**. It's **mine**.
It **belongs to** me.

Whose water bottle is this?
It's not **ours**. I think it's **hers**.

B PAIR WORK **Look at exercise 2B above again. Make sentences with *belong to* for each item and its owner(s).**

The water bottle belongs to …

C **Now go to page 129. Look at the grammar chart and do the grammar exercise for 1.2.**

D **Complete the conversations with the correct possessive form of the word in parentheses. Practice the conversations with a partner.**

1 A [1] Whose (who) water bottle is this?
B It isn't [2] ________ (I). Maybe it's [3] ________ (he).

2 A Sorry, which bag is [4] ________ (I)?
B That one is [5] ________ (you). And the other ones are [6] ________ (they).

4 SPEAKING

GROUP WORK **Choose three things from your pockets or bags and put them all together on one desk. Who do the different things belong to? Use possessives instead of names.**

OK, so, I think the tissues are yours.

Right! Whose mirror is this? Is it your mirror?

1.3 HOW DO YOU KNOW RAQUEL?

LESSON OBJECTIVE
- greet people and start a conversation

1 FUNCTIONAL LANGUAGE

A 1.06 **Look at the pictures. What is the connection between the people? Listen to the conversations and match them to the pictures. Are you right?**

A ☐

B ☐

1.06 Audio script

1 A Good morning! Are you Robert?
B Yes, I am.
A **Pleased to meet you.** I'm Julie, your coworker here.
B **Great to meet you, too.**
A I'm here to help. This is your desk, right here.
B Oh, OK. This is a nice office.
A **Do you know anybody here?**
B No, I don't.

2 A Hey, Raquel!
B Simon! **Long time, no see!** Please come in.
A **Great to see you again!**
B **It's really good to see you.**
B Oh, here's Patrick! Patrick, meet Simon.
A Hello, Patrick. **How do you know Raquel? Are you a friend of hers?**
C I'm her husband.

B **Complete the chart with expressions in bold from the conversations above.**

Greeting someone for the first time	Greeting someone who you know	Starting conversations
Good morning. Are you (Robert)? Pleased to [1] ________ ________. Great to meet you, [2] ________.	Long time, [3] ________ ________! [4] ________ to see you again! It's really [5] ________ to see you.	Do you [6] ________ anybody here? [7] ________ do you know (Raquel)? Are you a [8] ________ of hers / his / theirs?

C PAIR WORK **Greet your partner. Now change partners. Imagine you don't know your new partner, and greet them.**

2 REAL-WORLD STRATEGY

SHOWING INTEREST AND SURPRISE

You can use some common expressions to show interest and surprise.

Wow! *Seriously?*

Is it really? / Are you really?

A 1.07 **Read about showing interest and surprise in the box above. Use the expressions there to complete the conversation below. Listen to the full conversation and check.**

A Do you know anybody here?

B No, I don't. I'm pretty new to this city, too.

A [1] ______________ ? A new city *and* a new job – that's a lot! Well, that's Mr. Patel. He's the boss. His office is across from your desk.

B [2] ______________ ? That's good to know.

B PAIR WORK **Practice the conversation from exercise 2A, above.**

INSIDER ENGLISH

pretty = *beautiful*

*That's a **pretty** little house.*

pretty + **adjective** = *very*

*That's **pretty** good.* **(That's very good.)**

3 PRONUNCIATION: Saying /l/ at the end of a word

A 1.08 **Listen. Focus on the /l/ sounds. Practice saying the words.**

1 You look wonderfu**l**. 2 Beautifu**l** weather, isn't it? 3 How do you know Rache**l**?

B 1.09 **Listen. Who pronounces the /l/ sound at the end of the words clearly? Write A or B.**

1 beautiful B
2 bottle ___
3 full ___
4 girl ___
5 people ___
6 couple ___

C PAIR WORK **Say the words in exercise B to your partner. Does your partner say the /l/ sound?**

4 SPEAKING

A PAIR WORK **Read the situations. Then put the conversations in order. Read them with a partner.**

Situation 1: You're at a conference. Greet people you don't know.

- [ ] Good to meet you, too. Do you know anybody here?
- [ ] I'm Diana Reyes. Great to meet you.
- [ ] No, it's my first time at this conference.
- [1] Hello. I'm Daniel Santiago.

Situation 2: You arrive at a coffee shop to meet people you know.

- [ ] I know! Great to see you again!
- [1] Hi, Akram.
- [ ] Yeah, you, too. Hey, this is a nice place.
- [ ] Hi, Lola. Long time, no see!
- [ ] Yeah, isn't it?

B **Choose one of the conversations and add more to it. Use the language from this lesson. Then act out your conversation for the class.**

1.4 EMAIL INTRODUCTIONS

LESSON OBJECTIVE

- introduce yourself in an email

1 READING

A PAIR WORK **How many emails do you write in a month? Why do you write them? Do you write emails in English? Tell your partner.**

B READ FOR MAIN IDEAS **Read the email and choose the main idea.**

- [ ] He wants a job.
- [ ] He wants information about food.
- [ ] He wants cooking lessons.

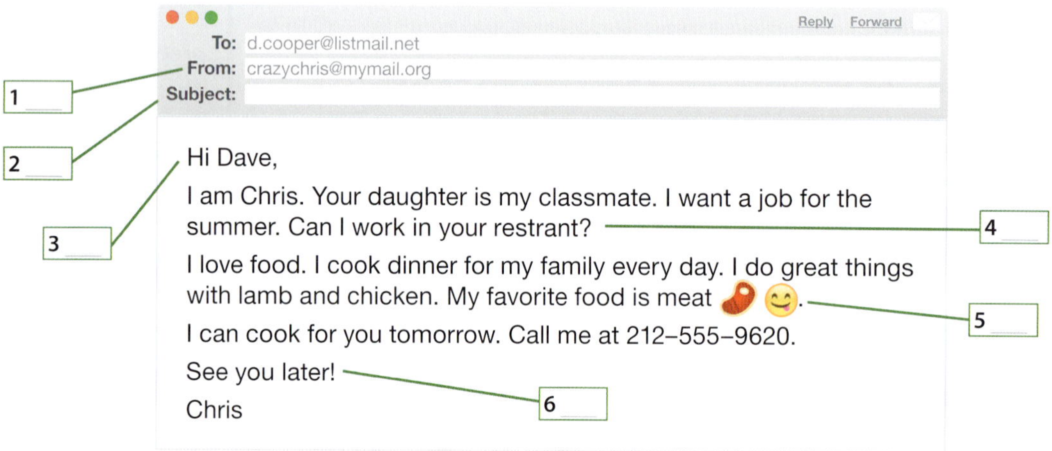
Reply Forward

To: d.cooper@listmail.net

From: crazychris@mymail.org

Subject:

Hi Dave,

I am Chris. Your daughter is my classmate. I want a job for the summer. Can I work in your restrant?

I love food. I cook dinner for my family every day. I do great things with lamb and chicken. My favorite food is meat.

I can cook for you tomorrow. Call me at 212-555-9620.

See you later!

Chris

C READ FOR DETAIL **There are problems with Chris's email. Read the comments (A–F) and match them with the correct part of the email.**

A What is your email about? You need a subject!

B Begin a formal sentence with *Dear Ms. / Mrs. / Mr. (last name)* or just *Dear Hiring Manager* or *Dear (job title)*. It's not a good idea to begin with *Hello, Hi,* or *Dear Friend*. You're not a friend!

C End the email with *Best wishes* or *All the best* and write your full name.

D A funny email address is OK for friends but not for people you don't know.

E Check your writing before you send your email.

F Don't use emojis in a formal email.

D **Read the Register check box and correct the problem in Chris's email.**

E 1.10 PAIR WORK THINK CRITICALLY **Listen to Dave's response to Chris's email. Does Dave offer Chris a job? Why not? What research do you need to do before you ask someone for a job? Discuss with your partner.**

REGISTER CHECK

In formal writing, don't write *I want ...*

A polite way to say what you want is *I would like ...*

2 WRITING

A Read the email. Does the writer follow the advice from the comments on page 8?

B **WRITING SKILLS** Look at the email again and circle the capital letters. Write the words with capital letters.

a pronoun (*I, you, he, she*, etc.) ______ I

b the beginning of a sentence ______

c names (people and organizations) ______

d titles (*Mr., Dr., Prof.*) ______

e places (countries, nationalities, towns) ______

f days of the week, months ______

Reply Forward

To: r.johnson65@listmail.net

From: lilymartin@mymail.org

Subject: Internship – Lily Martin

Dear Mr. Johnson,

Your daughter Abigail is my classmate at the University of Toronto.

In October and November every year, students in our class do an **internship**. I would like to do an internship in your company, Grallen Technologies. I attach my résumé to this email.

Thank you very much for your time.

Best wishes,

Lily Martin

GLOSSARY

internship (*n*) a period of time that a young person works in a company to get experience in a job

C Rewrite the email below with capital letters in the correct places.

Reply Forward

dear ms. ali,

my name is amanda barron. i work with your sister at first city bank in salvador. now i would like a new job.

can we meet on tuesday and talk about your company?

sincerely,

amanda barron

WRITE IT

D Think of a situation and write a formal email to someone you don't know. Include a connection to someone you both know and the reason for writing. Look at the examples in this lesson for help.

E **PAIR WORK** Exchange emails with another student. Write a reply.

1.5 TIME TO SPEAK
Things you have in common

LESSON OBJECTIVE
- talk about what you have in common

A **DECIDE** **Answer the questions with what you think. (Answers are at the bottom of the page.) Are you surprised?**

1 Imagine you have a group of 23 people. What is the probability that two people have the same birthday?
 a 50% b 23% c 0.056%

2 Imagine you have a group of 30 people. What is the probability that two people have the same birthday?
 a 25% b 70% c 4%

3 Now imagine you have 60 people. What is the probability that two people have the same birthday?
 a 50% b 10% c 99%

B **AGREE** **Think of your answers to the questions below. Then ask and answer the questions in a small group. When you have something in common with another person, put a check (✓).**

- When is your birthday? ☐
- How many brothers and sisters do you have? ☐
- What is your favorite possession? ☐
- Are you the first/second/third-born child? ☐
- What city are your parents from? ☐
- Where are your grandparents from? ☐
- What's in your bag? ☐
- Who's your favorite famous person? ☐
- How many friends do you have on Facebook? ☐

C **Count the checks in your group. Tell the class what you and the others in the group have in common. How many people have the same birthday in your group? In the class?**

D **DISCUSS** **Work in groups of four. Find more things you have in common and write the information below. Use the questions and phrases at the bottom of the page to help you.**

1 Everyone ____________________
2 Three people ____________________
3 Two people ____________________
4 One person ____________________

E **PRESENT** **Read your sentences to the class. Don't say the names! Can they guess who the people are?**

To check your progress, go to page 153.

Answers: 1 a 2 b 3 c

USEFUL PHRASES

DECIDE
I think …
Because …
Do you agree?

AGREE
Me, too! / Same here!
Not me. / I don't.

DISCUSS
What's your favorite … ?
Do you like … ?
What's your … called?
How many … do you have?
Do you have a/an … ?
When is … ?
Where are your … from?

UNIT OBJECTIVES

- talk about what you do every day, on the weekend, etc.
- talk about your workspace
- explain communication problems
- write your opinion about a podcast
- give advice about useful apps for work and study

WORK AND STUDY

2

START SPEAKING

A **Look at the picture. Who are the people? Where are they?**

B **Are you a very busy person? How do you remember all your plans? For example, do you use the calendar on your phone or do you write them down?**

C **Is this a busy week for you? Watch Allison's video.**

Is your busy day the same as Allison's?

2.1 KNOW YOUR NUMBERS

LESSON OBJECTIVE
- talk about what people do every day, on the weekend, etc.

1 LANGUAGE IN CONTEXT

A **Julia has a new fitness tracker. Read the article. Check (✓) the things it gives her information about.**

- [ ] class schedule
- [ ] drinking
- [ ] eating
- [ ] exercise
- [ ] free-time activities
- [ ] sleep
- [ ] study time
- [ ] the weather
- [ ] work

My life in NUMBERS

What do I know about my life? A lot more with my new **fitness tracker**.

Now I know I take 7,000 steps a day – not bad, but not great. But I also know that I look at my laptop for 10.5 hours every day! About 78% of that time (8.2 hours) is for work. When I have free time, I chat with friends (64 messages a day) or make plans for later.

I only sleep six hours a night (25%). Then I have something to drink (coffee or soda) about eight times a day to stay awake. Thank you, caffeine!!

The good news? I exercise a lot because I do a lot of housework (my roommate doesn't do anything). I do the laundry, the cooking, and the dishes, and I make the bed. That's about the same as walking 7.5 kilometers a day!

Learn your numbers with a **fitness tracker**! It can teach you a lot about you!

fitness tracker

GLOSSARY
step (*n*) a movement you make with your feet when you walk

B **Read Julia's article again. Does Julia need extra exercise? Why or why not?**

C **Do you think information like this is useful? Why or why not?**

2 VOCABULARY: Expressions with *do*, *have*, and *make*

A 1.11 **Listen and say the phrases. How many of these phrases are in the article?**

B **Now do the vocabulary exercises for 2.1 on page 142.**

C PAIR WORK **Which activities in exercise 2A do you usually do every day? Do you and your partner do the same things? Watch Celeste's video.**

REAL STUDENT

Do you do the same activities as Celeste?

3 GRAMMAR: Simple present for habits and routines

A **Complete the rules below. Use the sentences in the grammar box to help you.**

1 In affirmative sentences, add the letter ____________ to the verb when you talk about *he/she/it*.

2 In negative sentences, use *I don't* and *you don't*, but *he* or *she* ____________ .

3 For questions, add the letters ____________ to *do* when you ask about he/she/it.

4 For information questions, the question word (*what*, *when*, *where*, *who*, *why*, *how*) is before *do* or ____________ .

Simple present for habits and routines

I **do** the laundry and the cooking	My roommate **doesn't do** anything.	**Do** you **do** the laundry?
Julia **sleeps** six hours a night.	Julia **doesn't need** more exercise.	**Does** Julia **sleep** a lot?

Information questions

What does Julia **know** about her life?

How many steps do you **take** every day?

How often do you **have** something to drink?

B **Now go to page 130. Look at the grammar chart and do the grammar exercise for 2.1.**

C **Put the words in the right order to make questions and answers. Then check your accuracy.**

1 A day / does / start / usually / When / your
  B at / It / starts / usually / 7:00 a.m.

2 A coffees / day / do / every / have / How / many / you
  B cups / day / every / four / have / I

3 A dishes / do / do / How / often / the / you
  B dishes / do / evening / every / I / the

4 A does / family / dinner / have / time / What / your
  B at / eat / seven / usually / We

5 A do / hours / How / many / sleep / you
  B always / for / hours / I / seven / sleep

ACCURACY CHECK

Put these frequency words before the verb: *usually, often, never, sometimes*

Put other time phrases at the end of the sentence: *every day, every evening*

I do housework ~~usually~~ on Saturdays. ✗
I usually do housework on Saturdays. ✓

4 SPEAKING

PAIR WORK **Ask and answer the five questions from exercise 3C. Give answers that are true for you.**

2.2 WHERE'S YOUR WORKSPACE?

LESSON OBJECTIVE
- talk about your workspace

1 VOCABULARY: Naming work and study items

A **Do you usually use pen and paper, a computer, your phone, or a tablet at work or school? Why?**

B 1.12 **Look at the pictures. Listen and say the words. Which things do you use every day?**

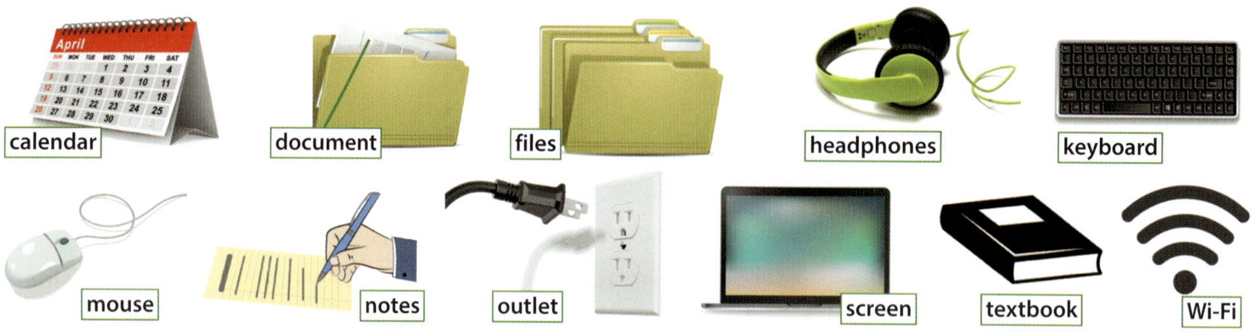

C **Now do the vocabulary exercises for 2.2 on page 142.**

2 LANGUAGE IN CONTEXT

A **Where do you like to work or study? Choose from these places. Why do you like to work or study there?**

at home at school in a café in a library in a park in an office

B 1.13 **Listen to three people talk about their favorite workspaces. Match the speakers to the pictures. Listen again and read to check.**

1.13 Audio script

1 This is my office. Well, kind of. There are lots of tables here. These small ones on the left are my favorite. I often have meetings in here, and there's lots of space to sit and see the same **screen**. There's free **Wi-Fi**, and the coffee is excellent, too!

2 Where do I work? In the spring and summer, I like to sit under these trees. All my **notes** and **files** and **textbooks** are on my laptop, so I don't need anything else. That's a mall over there, so I can have something to drink or a snack when I want.

3 This is where I usually study. I live a long way from school, so I'm here for two hours every day. Do you see that seat with the table, on the left? That's my favorite one. It's always quiet – I listen to music with my **headphones**. There's an electrical **outlet** between the seats.

A ☐

B ☐

C ☐

C PAIR WORK **Discuss the workspaces in the pictures. What's good and bad about them? Are these places better than the other places in exercise 2A? Why or why not?**

3 GRAMMAR: *This / that one; these / those ones*

A **Look at the pictures and complete the sentences with *this one*, *that one*, *these ones*, or *those ones*.**

1 ________________ are my favorites.

2 I like ________________ in the corner.

3 ________________ are very small.

4 ________________ has an electrical outlet.

B **Complete the rules with *one* or *ones*.**

1 Use *this* or *that* ________________ to talk about a singular thing that is near (*this*) or far (*that*).

2 Use *these* or *those* ________________ to talk about plural things that are near (*these*) or far (*those*).

C **Now go to page 131. Do the grammar exercise for 2.2.**

> **!** **Use *this, that, these,* and *those* with or without a noun.**
> ***This table***'s my favorite. ***This*** is my favorite table.
> ***One*** **and** ***ones*** **replace a noun.**
> *This* ***table***'s my favorite. *This* ***one***'s my favorite.

D **Look at the picture and complete the conversation with *this*, *that*, *these*, *those*, *one*, or *ones*.**

A Is [1] ___this___ a drawing of your office?

B Yes, it is. [2] ________________ is my desk here, in the corner.

A What's [3] ________________ green thing here? And what are [4] ________________ ones on the round table there?

B This green one is my chair, and those [5] ________________ are more chairs.

A And [6] ________________ things on your desk, what are they?

B [7] ________________ are my files and documents. And those [8] ________________ there on the table are more files.

A And what's [9] ________________ pink thing there?

B A place for books. Books I never look at!

4 SPEAKING

A PAIR WORK **Draw <u>your</u> usual work or study space. Ask and answer questions about it with your partner. Use the questions in the box.**

Where is this?	What's this here?	What's that over there?	What's that one?
Where is that?	What's this/that?	What are those/these?	Is this/that your laptop?

OK, so where's this?

This is where I usually work.

Is that your desk there?

No, this one's my desk, here. And that's my laptop.

B GROUP WORK **What do you like about your workspace and your partner's workspace? What don't you like? Tell your group.**

2.3 THE CONNECTION'S TERRIBLE

LESSON OBJECTIVE

- explain communication problems

1 FUNCTIONAL LANGUAGE

A 1.14 **Look at the communication problems in the box. Can you think of any more? Read and listen to the conversations. What communication problems do they have?**

a bad connection | no battery | no picture | problems hearing | someone speaking too fast

1.14 Audio script

1 **A** Hi, Hannah.
B Hi there, Pedro. How are you?
A Can you say that again? I can see you, but **I can't hear you very well.**
B Really? That's strange, I can hear you just fine, but I can't see you.
A Sorry, I lost you. What was that?
B I can't see you.
A Maybe **it's my Wi-Fi. Is that any better?**
B No, **the connection's terrible. We can try again later.**
A Fine, let's do that. Talk to you later.

2 **A** Hi, Hannah. **Can you hear me now?**
B Sorry, **you're breaking up.** Pedro, **are you still there?**
A Yes, still here, … but **there's an echo** now.
B Uh, … OK, wait. **Let me turn up the volume. How about now?**
A No, no better, sorry.
B **Let me call you, OK?**
A What? I didn't catch that.
B Let me call you.
A No, still nothing. I know! Let me call you.

B **Complete the chart with the expressions in bold from the conversations above.**

INSIDER ENGLISH

When you can't hear someone because of a bad connection, you *lose* them.

*Sorry, I **lost** you. I **lost** you there for a few seconds.*

Explaining the problem	Checking the problem	Solving the problem
I can't hear you very well.	Is that any better?	We can try again later.
It's my [1] ___ .	Can you [5] ___ me now?	Let me turn up the [8] ___ .
The [2] ___ 's terrible.	How [6] ___ ?	Let me [9] ___ , OK?
You're [3] ___ .	Are you [7] ___ ?	
There's an [4] ___ now.		

C PAIR WORK **Practice the conversations in exercise 1A with your partner.**

2 REAL-WORLD STRATEGY

ASKING FOR REPETITION

Use these expressions when you can't hear or understand what someone says.

Sorry, can you say that again?

Could you repeat that?

What? I didn't catch that.

______

A **Read the expressions in the box above. Find one more example on page 16 and add it to the box.**

B 1.15 **Complete the conversations using the expressions in the box. Then listen and check. Practice them with a partner.**

A

A Sorry, I lost you. Can you [1] ______ ?

B Yes, it's the hotel's Wi-Fi – it's terrible!

A Sorry, I [2] ______ .

B The hotel Wi-Fi is terrible!

B

A Sorry, [3] ______ that? The traffic noise is terrible.

B I said, "I'm running out of battery."

A Oh, OK. We can try again later.

3 PRONUNCIATION: Saying /h/ at the beginning of a word

A 1.16 **Listen. Write the missing words. Which sound do they all have?**

A [1] ______ there, Pedro. [2] ______ are you?

B [3] ______ , [4] ______ . Can you [5] ______ me now?

B 1.17 **Listen. Circle the words you hear.**

1 Hi! / eye
2 hear / ear
3 how / Ow!
4 head / Ed
5 his / is
6 hate / eight
7 Hannah / Anna
8 hat / at

C 1.18 **Listen and repeat. Focus on the /h/ sounds.**

1 I can't **h**ear you. The **h**otel's Wi-Fi is terrible.
2 I **h**ave **h**eadphones at **h**ome.
3 Can you **h**ear me OK? **H**ow about now?
4 I **h**ate **h**ousework!

4 SPEAKING

PAIR WORK **Choose a situation with your partner. Student A: Go to page 157. Student B: Go to page 159. Follow the instructions.**

Situations

- worker (A) to boss (B)
- student (A) to student (B)
- coworker (A) to coworker (B)
- student (A) to teacher (B)

2.4 HOW TO BE SUCCESSFUL

LESSON OBJECTIVE
- write your opinion about a podcast

1 LISTENING

A **Look at the title of the book. What are the habits of effective people, do you think? Here are some ideas.**

- ☐ clothes
- ☐ hobbies, interests, and sports
- ☐ food and drink
- ☐ ways of thinking
- ☐ sleeping habits

B 1.19 LISTEN FOR GIST **Listen to a podcast about the ideas in the book. Put the topics in exercise 1A in the order you hear them (1–4). There is one topic that isn't in the podcast.**

C 1.19 LISTEN FOR DETAILS **Listen to the podcast again and match the names to what the people usually do.**

1 Sergey Brin ___
2 Warren Buffett ___
3 Tim Cook ___
4 Seth Godin ___
5 Sheryl Sandberg ___

A ☐

B ☐

C ☐

D ☐

E ☐

FIND IT

D 1.20 PAIR WORK **What do you know about the people in exercise 1C? Where do they work, or how do they make money? Discuss with a partner. You can go online to find out more. Listen and check your ideas.**

E PAIR WORK THINK CRITICALLY **Answer the questions.**

1 Is it a good idea to copy the habits of successful people? Why or why not?
2 Why do you think *The 7 Habits of Highly Effective People* and similar books are so popular? Who do you think buys these books?

2 PRONUNCIATION: Listening for contractions

A 1.21 **Listen. Write the missing letters.**

1 **There'**___ a book called *The 7 Habits of Highly Effective People.*
2 **Can'**___ you tell us what they do?
3 They **don'**___ wear normal clothes.

B 1.22 **Complete the sentences with the three bold words from exercise 2A. Listen and check.**

1 ___________ has the same vowel sound as *coat*.
2 ___________ often sounds stronger than *can*.
3 ___________ often comes before *a* or *an*. The /z/ sound at the end connects to *a*.

3 WRITING

A Read the comments about the podcast. Then circle (A, B, or C).

1 A B C does not think that we can learn a lot from people's daily routines.

2 A B C gives information about the daily routine of another successful person.

3 A B C wants information about the daily routine of another successful person.

PODCAST **CHAT**

Profile Log out

A

The podcast is very interesting, but why are all these examples of businesspeople in America? There are other successful people – people from other countries, artists and creative people, more women. I would like to know about Viviane Senna, **for example**. What does she do every day on a normal day? We never read about her personal life.

B

Warren Buffett plays the ukulele? Give me a break! This is NOT a reason for his success. **I don't believe** we can learn anything from this information. The only important thing is the way people think.

C

Another example is Jack Dorsey of Twitter. He does the same things every day. He gets up at 5:00 a.m. and meditates for 30 minutes, exercises, and then has his first coffee. On the weekend, he plays sports, and he thinks about the next week. **Like all the others** in the podcast, he's really successful.

B WRITING SKILLS **Look at the phrases in bold in the comments above. Match each phrase to a category.**

1 Giving an opinion ______

2 Giving an example ______

3 Comparing ______

WRITE IT

C Write a comment of 40–60 words about the podcast. Use the comments in exercise 3A and the phrases in exercise 3B to help you. You can:

- Give your opinion of the podcast.
- Give an example of the daily routines of a successful person you know.
- Compare one of these successful people to another successful person you know.

D There are spelling mistakes in some of the words below. Correct the mistakes. Then check your spelling in exercise 3C.

belive ______	poeple ______
businesspeople ______	personal ______
exercise ______	realy ______
intresting ______	successful ______

E Read the comments of other students in your class. Choose one comment that you think is interesting and write a short reply.

2.5 TIME TO SPEAK
Apps for life

LESSON OBJECTIVE
- give advice about useful apps for work and study

USE IT

A Look at the different categories of apps on the right. Which ones do you have on your phone? Which ones do you use every day? Why do you like them? Does your partner use the same apps?

B Read what the students say, and give advice on apps useful for them.

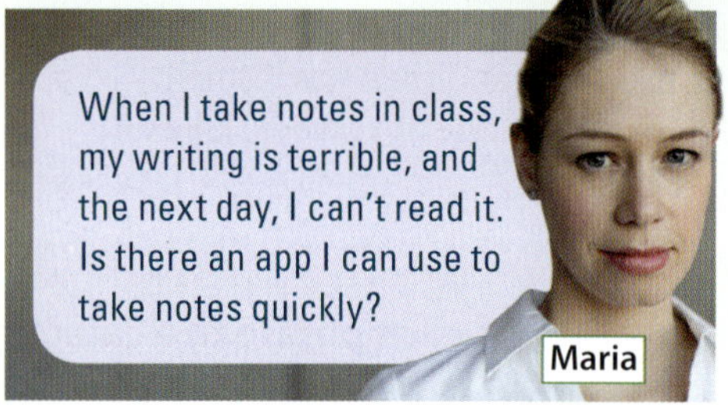

C **DISCUSS** Think about what types of apps you would like to help you study English. Discuss in your group. Use the phrases at the bottom of the page to help you.

D **DECIDE** Your school wants to give a "welcome pack" of four smartphone or tablet apps to new students. Choose four apps from your phones and say why they are useful.

E **PRESENT** Tell the class about your group's suggestions. Listen to the other suggestions. Write down any apps that you think are useful for you.

F Tell your partner which apps from today you'd like to download, and why. How are you going to use the apps?

To check your progress, go to page 153.

USEFUL PHRASES

DISCUSS
I want to … / I'd like to …
I find it hard to …
Is there an app I can use to … ?
How does it work?
Why do you like it?

DECIDE
My advice is …
Let's choose this app because …

PRESENT
We think this is a great/helpful/fun app.
We like this app because …

UNIT OBJECTIVES

- talk about what you're doing at the moment
- talk about sports and exercise
- ask for information
- write short messages to a company
- create a fitness program

LET'S MOVE

3

START SPEAKING

A What are the people in the picture doing? Is this a good picture to represent sports?

B Which big sports events do you like to watch on TV? Why do you like them?

C How important are sports for you or in your country? Explain your reasons. For ideas, watch Irene's video.

REAL STUDENT

Are sports in your country the same as in Irene's country?

3.1 WE'RE WINNING!

LESSON OBJECTIVE

- talk about what you're doing at the moment

1 VOCABULARY: Sports

A 1.23 **Look at the pictures. What sports do you see? Work with a partner and match the pictures to the words. Listen and say the words.**

athlete	court	fans	field	goal	gym
lose	~~player~~	pool	race	team	win

1 player
2 ______

3 ______

4 ______

5 ______

6 ______

7 ______

8 ______

9 ______

10 ______
11 ______

12 ______

B **Are the words above (a) events, (b) people, (c) places, or (d) results. Make four lists. Add one more word to each list.**

C **Now do the vocabulary exercises for 3.1 on page 142.**

D PAIR WORK **Which sports do you play? Where do you watch sports?**

2 LANGUAGE IN CONTEXT

A **Read about the action in two sports events: a soccer game and a tennis game . Circle the correct sport in each update.**

SPORTS LIVE

a) The 45,000 Brazilian and 35,000 Uruguayan **fans** are incredible! They're making a lot of noise. Here come the **players**.

b) Gomez **loses** the first game of this final. It's getting hot here on the **court**: 33°C. The world number one isn't playing well today.

c) 1–0! Fantastic **goal**! Uruguay is **winning**! The Brazilian players can't believe it.

d) Gomez wins the second game, but something's wrong. What's he doing now? He's calling a doctor onto the court.

e) Wait, it's not a goal! No goal! Now the Uruguayan team can't believe it. Everyone is on the **field**. It's crazy!

f) Gomez is leaving the court. He's crying. It's a terrible end to the game for this star **athlete**.

B **Read the SportsLive updates again. In which sport …**

a is a player hurt? ______ **b** is it a final? ______ **c** are there lots of people? ______

3 GRAMMAR: Present continuous

A **Circle the correct option to complete the rule. Use the sentences in the grammar box to help you.**

We use the present continuous for actions that happen **usually or all the time / right now.**

Present continuous

It**'s getting** hot here on the court.	What **is** he **doing** now?
The world number one **isn't playing** well today.	Gomez **is leaving** the court.

B **Now go to page 131. Look at the grammar chart and do the grammar exercise for 3.1.**

C PAIR WORK **What are the fans doing in the picture? Find five things. Tell your partner.**

4 SPEAKING

A **Read the conversation. Why is Kate calling Pedro?**

Pedro Where are you?

Kate I'm in a restaurant. And guess what! Ronaldo is sitting at the table right next to me! Ronaldo!

Pedro Really? What's he doing?

Kate He's eating a sandwich!

Pedro No way! Take a picture.

INSIDER ENGLISH

Say *Guess what!* when you have something interesting or surprising to say, and you want someone to really listen.

B **Imagine you're in a restaurant and you see a famous athlete. Think of answers to these questions.**

Where are you? Who can you see? Who is he/she with? What are they doing?

C PAIR WORK **Call your partner to tell them about your famous person from exercise 4B. Use the conversation in exercise 4A as a model.**

3.2 THE 16TH STEP

LESSON OBJECTIVE
- talk about sports and exercise

1 LANGUAGE IN CONTEXT

A

B

C

A **Look at the pictures. What sports do you see?**

B 1.24 **Listen to the podcast. Which picture from exercise 1A are they talking about?**

C 1.24 **Listen again and read. Why is Lex on the Paralympic team? What does he do that you can't?**

1.24 Audio script

Tyler Do you exercise much?

Bree I **stretch** every morning when I wake up. I **climb** the stairs to come here. And now I'm **lifting** my coffee cup.

Tyler Seriously? Well, today we're talking about a real athlete: Lex Gillette.

Bree I think I know that name.

Tyler Yes. He's amazing! He has four Paralympic silver medals for long jump.

Bree Wow!

Tyler Yeah – and he's blind.

Bree What? You mean he can run and **jump**, but he can't see? How does he do it?

Tyler He practices more than 30 hours a week.

Bree Really? Hey, maybe he's jumping right now!

Tyler I don't think so. It's early, so I think he's probably stretching now. Athletes stretch a lot, and they usually go to the gym and **lift** weights.

Bree But Lex can't see, so how does he do the long jump?

Tyler When he runs, he knows the number of steps to take: 16. On the 16th step, he jumps.

Bree That's scary! But it's awesome!

D PAIR WORK **Which sports from exercise 1 do you like to do? Imagine you are blind. Can you do the sports well? What problems does a blind athlete have?**

2 VOCABULARY: Exercising

A 1.25 **Listen and say the words. What two activities are the people doing in the pictures on page 24?**

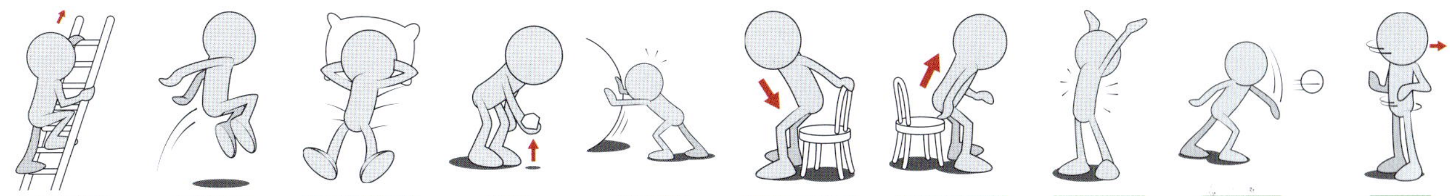

climb | jump | lie down | lift | push | sit down | stand up | stretch | throw | turn

B PAIR WORK **Look at the activities. Describe the routine to a partner. For ideas, watch Celeste's video.**

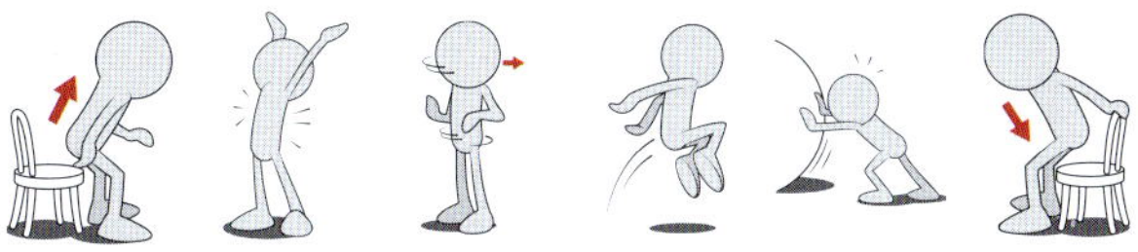

Stand up. Now stretch your arms.

REAL STUDENT

Whose routine is more difficult? Yours or Celeste's?

C **Now do the vocabulary exercises for 3.2 on page 143.**

3 GRAMMAR: Simple present and present continuous

A **Circle the correct options to complete the rules. Use the sentences in the grammar box to help you.**

Use the simple present when actions happen **usually / at the time of speaking**.

Use the present continuous when actions happen **usually / at the time of speaking**.

Simple present and present continuous

Do you **exercise** much?	I'**m lifting** my coffee cup.
I stretch every morning	He'**s jumping** right now.

ACCURACY CHECK

Use the *-ing* form of the verb with the present continuous.

I'm ~~watch~~ the game now. ✗

I'm watching the game now. ✓

B **Now go to page 132. Do the grammar exercise for 3.2.**

C **Put the verbs in the correct form. Then check your accuracy.**

A I _'m thinking_ (think) of a famous soccer player.

B Where [1] ______ (he / come) from?

A He [2] ______ (come) from Brazil, but right now he [3] ______ (live) in Spain.

B [4] ______ (he / play) in the game on TV right now?

A No, he [5] ______ (not be).

D PAIR WORK **Think of a famous athlete, but don't tell your partner. Ask questions to guess your partner's famous athlete.**

4 SPEAKING

A **Think of a friend you know who exercises a lot. Prepare answers to these questions.**

What kind of exercise does he/she do?

Why does he/she like this activity?

How often does he/she exercise or play sports?

What is he/she probably doing right now?

B GROUP WORK **Talk about your friends. Ask and answer the questions in exercise 4A and think of three more questions.**

3.3 COULD YOU TELL ME ... ?

LESSON OBJECTIVE
- ask for information

A

B

1 FUNCTIONAL LANGUAGE

A **Look at the pictures. What places do you see?**

B 1.26 **Read and listen. In conversation 1, why doesn't the police officer know where he can buy a T-shirt? In conversation 2, do you think the man buys the T-shirt? Why or why not?**

1.26 Audio script

1 A Excuse me. **We're looking for** section C.
B Section C is … over there, I think.
A Thanks. **Do you know** when the game starts?
B Seven-thirty.
A Great. One more thing. **Could you tell me** where I can get a T-shirt?
B I'm not sure. I don't work here. Try the store.
A OK. Thank you.

2 A Excuse me. **I'm looking for** a large T-shirt.
B All the T-shirts are over there. The large shirts are on the right.
A I see them, thanks. Um, **do you know** the price of this white shirt? There's no price tag.
B Sure. This one is $55.
A Oh! OK, thank you.

C **Complete the chart with expressions in bold from the conversations above.**

Asking for information

Excuse me.
We're [1] ____________ (section C).
I'm [2] ____________ (a large T-shirt).
Could [3] ____________ where I can get (a T-shirt)?
Do [4] ____________ (when the game starts)?
Do [5] ____________ (the price of this white shirt)?

D 1.27 **Complete the conversations. Then listen and check. Practice with a partner.**

1 A Excuse me. *Could you tell me / I'm looking for* what time the gym closes? B At nine-thirty.
2 A *I'm looking for / Do you know* the way to court number three? B Sure. It's over there.

2 REAL-WORLD STRATEGY

A 1.28 **Listen to another conversation in the store. What information does the woman ask for?**

B 1.28 **Listen again and circle what the woman does when she doesn't understand.**

a She repeats his words as a question. b She tells him she doesn't understand.

CHECKING INFORMATION

To check information you don't understand, you can repeat words as questions.

Do you want a bag for that? They're ***five cents.***

Sorry? ***Five cents?***

The bag, for the T-shirt. It's ***five cents.***

C 1.29 **Read about checking information in the box. Then listen to the questions and respond after the beep to check information.**

1 **A** Could you tell me where the away fans sit?

B Sorry, the *away fans*?

A Yes, the fans of the visiting team.

D PAIR WORK **Student A: Go to page 157. Student B: Go to page 159. Follow the instructions.**

3 PRONUNCIATION: Saying /oʊ/ and /ɔ/ vowel sounds

A 1.30 **Listen to the words. Practice saying them. Do you make the /oʊ/ and /ɔ/ sounds?**

/oʊ/ know /ɔ/ store

B 1.31 **Listen and write the words you hear. Which words have the /oʊ/ sound? Which ones have the /ɔ/ sound?**

C **Work with a partner. Practice the conversations.**

A Is this the door to the sports hall? **B** I'm not sure. I think it's the door to the courts.

A Can you show me the photos of your store. **B** Sure. Here are four photos. Do you want more?

4 SPEAKING

A PAIR WORK **Put the conversation in order. Then practice it.**

- ☐ There's a machine outside the class. It sells water.
- 1 Excuse me. I'm looking for the fitness class.
- ☐ Sure. It's on the second floor. Take the stairs – the elevator's out of order.
- ☐ Sorry? Out of order?
- ☐ It finishes at 9:00, I think.
- ☐ 9:00? Great. Just one more thing. Do you know where I can get some water?
- ☐ Yes, it doesn't work. You need to take the stairs.
- ☐ Thank you!
- ☐ Ah! OK, out of order. Got it. Also, could you tell me what time the class finishes?

B PAIR WORK **Have a conversation with your partner using information about the swimming pool.**

3.4 BIKE SHARING

LESSON OBJECTIVE
- write short messages to a company

1 LISTENING

FIND IT

A **What is bike sharing? Is there a bike-sharing program in your city? You can go online to find out more about it. Would you like to ride a bike in a foreign city? Why or why not?**

B **Read the introduction to a podcast. Where is Jon? What is he doing?**

BICYCLE TRAVELER

New York, Paris, Rio — just three of the many big cities with a popular bike-sharing program. It's clear why these programs are popular: bike riding is a healthy, cheap, and fast way to travel in the city. But what is it like for a visitor? Our reporter Jon Davies spends a day in Mexico City and tries out the *EcoBici* program.

C 1.32 PREDICT **Before his bike ride, does Jon think it's a good idea? Do you think he feels the same after his ride? Listen and check.**

D 1.32 LISTEN FOR DETAIL **Listen again and answer the questions.**

1 Who usually uses the EcoBici program?
2 How does Marcello use the program?
3 What sometimes happens when cars turn right?
4 What is one problem with the program?
5 What does Marcello do when that happens?
6 How does Jon feel at the end of his ride?

E PAIR WORK THINK CRITICALLY **What are some positive and negative things about bike-sharing programs? Discuss with a partner. Do you think these programs are a good idea for every city? Why or why not?**

I think bike-sharing programs are good because you can get around town fast.

I don't think they're a good idea because sometimes there are no bikes at the docking stations.

2 PRONUNCIATION: Listening for linking sounds

A 1.33 **Listen to what Jon says. Focus on the words that link together when Jon says them. Practice saying the sentence slowly. Then say it more quickly. How quickly can you say it?**

Cycling‿in Mexico City‿is‿a great way to get around.

B 1.34 **Draw lines between the linking sounds. Listen and check.**

1 How are you feeling? 2 I'll watch out for that. 3 This is basically an enormous traffic jam.

C **Complete the rule.**

Consonant sounds at the *start / end* of a word usually connect to *consonant / vowel* sounds at the start of the next word.

3 WRITING

A **Read the messages. Where do you see messages like this? Which messages are positive, and which are negative?**

Tweets   Tweets & replies   Media

@citizenbrian I'm looking for a station near the pool, but I can NEVER find one, @citibikeride. 0 1

@davidbarts2 Hey @citibikeride, one of the bikes is broken and no power at the docking station. What do I do? 3 2

@thelittleone Hi @citibikeride, just to say THANK YOU for putting bikes outside my house. Now I can ride to school, yay! #ridinginthecity 1 11

@lulu Hi @citibikeride. No bikes at the station near the gym. We need more bikes there, please. 8 0

@lordaudifan Big bike station on my street, so no space for cars. Now I can't park. :-(Thanks a lot, @citibikeride. 1 2

REGISTER CHECK

In a text message or tweet, you can leave out words:

No bikes at the station.

When you write the same message as an email, use all the words.

***There are** no bikes at the station.*

B **WRITING SKILLS** **Look for the words *and*, *but*, and *so* in the messages above. Then complete the sentences.**

1 We use ________ to describe the result of an action.
2 We use ________ to add another item to a list of things.
3 We use ________ to present a different choice.

C **Match the two parts of the sentences.**

1 There are no bikes at the docking station, so
2 It's 45 minutes to work by bus, but
3 When I ride a bike, I exercise and

a by bike it's 20 minutes.
b I get there faster.
c I'm walking to the subway.

WRITE IT

D **Use two of your positive points and one of your negative points from exercise 1E on page 28 and write your own messages to the bike-sharing program. Don't forget to use *and*, *but*, and *so*.**

3.5 TIME TO SPEAK
Fitness programs

LESSON OBJECTIVE
- create a fitness program

FIND IT

A **RESEARCH** Look at the sports and fitness activities on the phone. Where are the people, and what are they doing? Read the information on the screen. Go online to find information about free sports and fitness activities where you live, if you can.

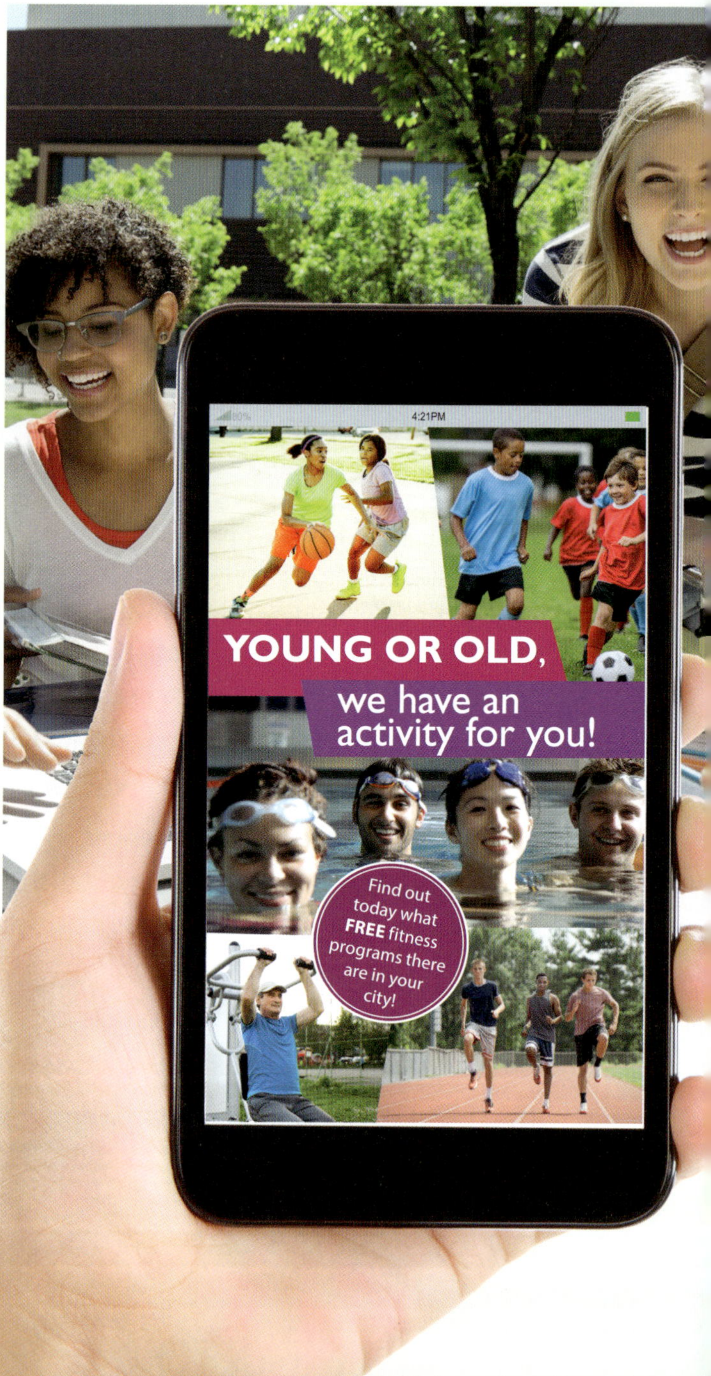

B **DISCUSS** What are the positive things about free fitness programs? What other types of free activities are usually available in a town? In a school? Use the phrases at the bottom of the page to help you.

C **PREPARE** Design a fitness program for your town, workplace, or school. Use your ideas from A and B. Think about …

- **activities** Choose four different activities.
- **location(s)** You can choose one place or a few.
- **timetable** When do people do these activities? How often do they do them?
- **people** Who is it for, and why?

D **PRESENT** Tell the class about your fitness program. Listen to the suggestions from the other groups. Which ideas do you like? Why?

E **AGREE** Your town can have two new fitness programs. Discuss which two programs to choose. Make a decision as a class.

To check your progress, go to page 153.

USEFUL PHRASES

DISCUSS

Free fitness programs are good because …

Free fitness programs help people to …

What do you think?

PREPARE

What about (soccer/swimming/tennis, etc.)?

Where can people do them?

What time is good for people/parents/ students?

How does it help?

PRESENT

Our program is called …

It helps people because …

Any questions?

REVIEW 1 (UNITS 1–3)

1 VOCABULARY

A **Read the words. Which word doesn't belong in each category? Circle it.**

1 People you know: grandson coworker girlfriend (player) classmate 6
2 Everyday things: boss keychain candy bar hand lotion umbrella ____
3 Expressions with *have*: a snack free time something to drink the laundry a party ____
4 Expressions with *do*: some work the laundry housework some coffee the dishes ____
5 Work and study: calendar textbook document push Wi-Fi ____
6 Sports words: court pool team screen race ____
7 Exercising: stretch cash throw jump turn ____

B **Look at the words you circled in exercise 1A. Where do those words really belong? Write the category number (1–7).**

C **Add three more words or phrases that you know to each category.**

2 GRAMMAR

A **Circle the correct words to complete the conversations.**

1 **A** What do you have in [1]*your / her* bag?
B [2]*The / My* sunglasses and [3]*my wife's umbrella / the umbrella of my wife.*
A Why? It [4]*doesn't rain / isn't raining* right now.
B No, it [5]*isn't / aren't*, but [6]*often it / it often* rains here in the fall.

2 **A** Who are [7]*that / these* people in the picture?
B Max and Sacha.
A I [8]*doesn't / don't* know them. [9]*Do / Does* they work with you?
B No, they [10]*isn't / aren't* my coworkers. They're my neighbors. They [11]*lives / live* next door.
A I see. And [12]*who / whose* head is that in the photo?
B Ha! It's mine!

B PAIR WORK **Practice reading the conversations.**

3 SPEAKING

PAIR WORK **Describe your routine to your partner. Ask and answer the questions.**

- What do you usually do during the week? And on the weekend?
- What are you doing today? Are you doing anything that is different from normal?

I usually work during the week. On weekends, I exercise or go to the gym. I love sports.

These days, I'm learning to play hockey. It's great!

4 FUNCTIONAL LANGUAGE

A **Circle the correct options to complete the conversation.**

A Hi, Carol. Long time no see!

B Hi, Leo. [1]*Nice to see you again! / nice to meet you!*

A How are you?

B I'm good. This is a great [2]*place / weather*, isn't it? The house is beautiful.

A Yeah, really great. It's my first time here. Do you know [3]*anybody / some person* here?

B I know everyone! It's my close friend's party.

A So, you know Max? [4]*Actually? / Seriously?* Wow! I know him from school. So, you know the house, too, right?

B Yeah.

A Good. Can you [5]*know / tell me* where the kitchen is? I'm really hungry.

B Me, too! Come on, it's this way.

B **Two friends are having problems with their connection. Complete their conversation with the verbs in the box.**

call	catch	hear	is	say	try

A Hi, can you [1] ________ me OK?

B No, the connection is terrible.

A OK, let me [2] ________ you. OK?

B Sorry, can you [3] ________ that again? I didn't [4] ________ that.

A I said, "Let me call you."

B OK, I'm sorry, it's my Wi-Fi.

A How about now? [5] ________ that any better?

B No, sorry. Let's [6] ________ again later.

5 SPEAKING

A PAIR WORK **Choose one of the situations. Act it out in pairs.**

1 You are at a party. Talk to somebody you don't know. Talk about the people at the party, the place, the weather, etc. Think of some surprising information to tell your partner.

A Hello, I'm [name].

B Hi, [name]. I'm [name]. Nice to meet you.

2 You are talking to a friend online. There is a problem with the internet connection. Explain the problem. Ask for repetition to check the problem. Decide what you are going to do to solve it.

A Hi, how are you doing? It's so nice to speak to you again.

B Hi! How are you? Listen, I can't hear you very well …

3 You are in a large sports store. You want to buy a souvenir of your favorite team. Ask the sales clerk for information about where to find things. Check the information before you finish the conversation.

A Excuse me, can you help us? We're looking for …

B Sure, all the souvenirs are …

B **Change roles and repeat the role play.**

UNIT OBJECTIVES

- talk about your plans
- talk about giving and receiving gifts
- make and respond to invitations
- write an online event announcement
- choose gifts for your host

GOOD TIMES

4

START SPEAKING

A **Look at the picture. What is happening? Do you think they're having a good time? Do you have similar events in your country?**

B **Which things are important for special events (for example, a cake for a birthday party)? Why? Can you think of other things connected to special occasions?**

cake	dancing	family
fireworks	food	friends
games	gifts	music

REAL STUDENT

Is your family celebration the same as Irene's?

C **What special days do you have with your family? What do you usually do? For ideas, watch Irene's video.**

4.1 COMIC CELEBRATION

LESSON OBJECTIVE
- talk about your plans

1 VOCABULARY: Describing pop culture

FIND IT

A 1.35 **What do you know about Comic Con? Look at the pictures. Which things can you find at Comic Con? You can go online to find out more. Listen and repeat the words.**

a **TV show**

fans playing **video games**

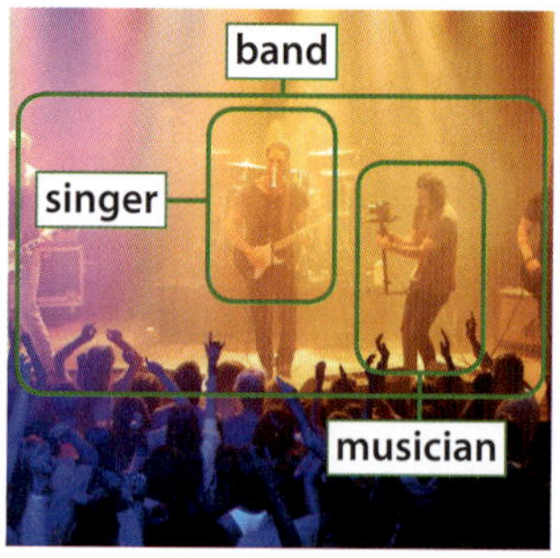

a **concert**

an arts **festival**

B PAIR WORK **With your partner, think of examples of these things.**

one famous artist	*two* popular video games	*three* TV shows
three movie actors	*four* bands / singers / musicians	*two* movie directors

C **Now do the vocabulary exercises for 4.1 on page 143.**

2 LANGUAGE IN CONTEXT

A **Read Cassie's blog post. Which words from exercise 1A does she use in her post?**

Fangirl Superhero

Blog About

So excited! Comic Con is coming here this weekend. Yay! Tommy and I have our new costumes, and they look totally cool!

Here's my Comic Con Top 3.

1. Movies! Don't miss the Star Trek celebration on Saturday. You can meet some of the actors and directors from the TV shows and movies. Can't wait! I'm bringing my camera, so check out next week's post for photos.

2. Games! The gaming hall is 2,000m^2 of games, games, and more games!

3. Art! Guess what? Tommy is showing his pictures at Artists' Alley this year. He isn't selling anything, but you can order from his website.

Are you going to Comic Con? What are you doing? Add a comment and tell me about it.

GLOSSARY

fangirl (*n*) a female fan who loves comics, films, and/or music

costume (*n*) clothes you wear to look like someone else

B **Read the blog again. Check (✓) the sentence(s) that are true. Correct the false ones.**

☐ 1 Cassie doesn't like her costume.

☐ 2 You can meet famous people from TV and movies.

☐ 3 Tommy wants to sell his pictures at Comic Con.

3 GRAMMAR: Present continuous for future plans

A **Circle the correct options to complete the rules. Use the sentences in the grammar box to help you.**

1 You **can** / **can't** use the present continuous for the future.

2 Use the present continuous for **plans or arrangements** / **predictions**.

Present continuous for future plans

Comic Con **is coming** this weekend. I'**m bringing** my camera. **Are** you **going** to Comic Con?

B **Now go to page 132. Look at the grammar chart and do the grammar exercise for 4.1.**

C 1.36 **Complete the sentences with the present continuous form of the verb in parentheses ( ). Listen and check. Then read the conversation in pairs.**

A What [1] ___are___ you ___doing___ (do) on Saturday?

B We [2] ____________ (go) to the music festival in the afternoon.

A Yeah? I [3] ____________ (go), too! My brother's band [4] ____________ (play).

B No way! When [5] ________ he ________ (play)?

A At 8:30, on the new music stage.

B Oh, no! We [6] ____________ (not stay) that long.

INSIDER ENGLISH

Say *No way!* when you're really surprised to hear something.

D PAIR WORK **Look at the activities. Ask and answer questions about this weekend with your partner.**

go to a concert | go to the movies | see friends | study | visit family | work

Are you going to the movies this weekend?

Yeah. We're seeing the new Star Wars movie.

4 SPEAKING

GROUP WORK **What is your group doing between this class and the next one? Find a time when you can all meet.**

What are you doing after class, Ricardo?

I'm meeting my sister for dinner.

Are you doing anything tomorrow?

Tomorrow? No, I'm free all day.

4.2 THE PERFECT GIFT

LESSON OBJECTIVE
- talk about giving and receiving gifts

1 VOCABULARY: Naming gift items

A 1.37 **Are you a difficult person to buy gifts for? Why? Look at the gifts. Listen and say the words. Which gifts would you like?**

B PAIR WORK **Imagine you are buying gifts for friends and family. Who would like each of these gifts?**

C **Now do the vocabulary exercises for 4.2 on page 144.**

2 LANGUAGE IN CONTEXT

A 1.38 **Listen to three people talking about gifts. Which gifts from exercise 1A does each person say?**

B 1.38 **Listen again and read. Why are these people difficult to buy gifts for?**

Lara's dad   Rosa and her brothers   Hasan's sister

1.38 Audio script

Lara It's really difficult to find a gift for my dad. He always tells me he doesn't want anything. In the end, I usually get him something boring like a **sweatshirt** or socks. This year I'm going for something a little different. I'm buying him an experience – a **gift card**, for one hour of driving a really fast sports car. I hope he likes it. It wasn't cheap!

Hasan My little sister's very difficult. I never know what gift to get her. I sometimes buy **perfume** or clothes for her, but she never likes them. Or I take her to a movie, but she doesn't want to watch it. This year I'm giving her a **bouquet of flowers**. Who doesn't like flowers?

Rosa Mom and dad never know what gifts to get for me and my brothers. They usually buy us books or a watch. This year we're asking them for gift cards. Then we can get what we really want in our favorite stores.

C 1.39 **Are the people happy when they get their gifts? Listen and check.**

3 GRAMMAR: Object pronouns

A **Read the sentences in the grammar box. Then find the people and things in the text on page 36 that the words in bold replace.**

Object pronouns

He always tells **me** he doesn't want anything.
I usually get **him** something boring.
I hope he likes **it**.
I never know what gift to get **her**.
I buy perfume or clothes, but she never likes **them**.
I take her to a movie, but she doesn't want to watch **it**.
Mom and dad never know what gifts to get for **me** and my brothers.
They usually buy **us** books or a watch.
This year we're asking **them** for gift cards.

B **Which object pronouns in the grammar box refer to:**

a people? ______ ______ ______ ______ ______

b objects? ______ ______

c both? ______

C **Now go to page 133. Look at the grammar chart and do the grammar exercise for 4.2.**

D **Replace the words in parentheses with object pronouns. Then check your accuracy. Tell your partner about the things you buy for the people in your family.**

1 My dad loves cooking. I always buy cookbooks for (my dad) ___him___. He loves (cookbooks) ______.

2 My sister is difficult to buy for. I usually get (my sister) ______ gift cards to her favorite stores. She likes (gift cards) ______ because she can choose the clothes she wants.

3 Music is my parents' passion. They love (music) ______! It's really easy to buy a gift for (my parents) ______.

ACCURACY CHECK

Use *it* or *them* after *like*.

Thank you, it's beautiful. I really ~~like~~! ✗

Thank you, it's beautiful. I really like it! ✓

4 SPEAKING

PAIR WORK **Imagine you want to buy some gifts. Choose three people you know and decide what to get for them. For ideas, watch Caio's video.**

- a neighbor – he/she often helps you
- your boss – it's his/her last day at work
- a teenager – he/she loves technology
- a young child – it's his/her birthday
- a close friend – he/she is feeling sad
- your teacher – a thank-you gift

I want to get something for my art teacher for her birthday.

How about a bouquet of flowers? She can paint a picture of them.

REAL STUDENT

Do you want to buy the same things as Caio?

4.3 I'D LOVE TO!

LESSON OBJECTIVE

- make and respond to invitations

1 FUNCTIONAL LANGUAGE

A 1.40 **Read and listen to the phone calls and voicemails. Where do the friends plan to meet? Where do they meet in the end?**

1.40 Audio script

A Hey Mika, are you doing anything later? We're going to that street festival downtown. **Would you like to** come?

B Oh, **sorry**, Daniel, **I can't. I wish I could, but** I'm working on my paper today.

A Come on! You can work on your paper later.

B That's true. OK. **I'd love to.**

A Great! **We can meet you** at three at the subway station.

B **See you there**!

(**3:00 p.m.**)

B Hi! I'm at the subway station. Where are you?

(**3:05 p.m.**)

A Sorry, Mika. Just got your message. We're running late. **Let's meet** at that new pizza place on Third Street. **See you soon.**

(**3:15 p.m.**)

B Hey, Daniel. It's me again. I'm outside the restaurant now. Are you guys close?

A We're here now. Where are you? Oh, wait, I can see you!

> **!** *a guy* = a man
> *That guy over there lives in my building.*
>
> *guys* = a group of people, any number, men and/or women
> *I'll meet you guys at the elevator in five minutes.*
> *Hey, guys! What's up?*

B **Complete the chart with expressions in bold from the conversation and voicemails above.**

Invite someone	Would you [1] ______ to (come)?
Accept	I'd [2] ______ to!
Don't accept	Sorry, Daniel, I [3] ______ . I [4] ______ I could, but (I'm working on my paper).
Suggest when and where to meet	We [5] ______ meet you (at a quarter after / at the subway). Let's [6] ______ (at the pizza place / later).
Agree on a plan	[7] ______ you there! See you [8] ______ .

C PAIR WORK **Practice the conversations and voicemails in exercise 1A with your partner.**

2 REAL-WORLD STRATEGY

A 1.41 **Listen to Lucca and Jen. Where does Lucca want to go? Does Jen want to go?**

MAKING GENERAL EXCUSES

When you don't want to accept an invitation because you have a lot to do, give a general reason followed by the suggestion of much more.

I don't know. I have homework ***and stuff.***

I'm not sure. I have family visiting ***and things.***

Maybe, but I'm getting ready to go on vacation ***and everything.***

B 1.41 **Read the information in the box above. Then listen again and complete Lucca and Jen's conversation with words from the box.**

Lucca Hi, Jen. What's up?

Jen Not much.

Lucca Are you doing anything later? We're going to the concert in the park.

Jen 1 ____________. I have work and then the gym 2 ____________.

Lucca Come on! It'll be fun.

Jen 3 ____________ next time.

C PAIR WORK **Imagine someone invites you to these events. Refuse the invitation and give a general excuse. Practice with your partner.**

- a music festival in the park on Saturday and Sunday
- a video game competition all day tomorrow, two hours from where you live
- a band at a local café tonight, 9:00 p.m. to midnight

3 PRONUNCIATION: Saying /v/ in the middle of a word

A 1.42 **Listen to the words. Focus on the /v/ sound. Practice saying the sound.**

1 love 2 have 3 everything 4 festival

B 1.43 **Listen. Who pronounces the /v/ sound? Circle** ***A*** **or** ***B*****.**

1 A Would you like to come to the street festival?
 B I'd love to.

2 A Hi Vivian! Do you want to go to the concert with us?
 B Sorry, I can't. I have work and everything.

3 A We're going to a video game competition. Would you like to come?
 B Sorry, I can't. I'm going to a music festival.

C **Practice the conversations in exercise 3B with a partner.**

4 SPEAKING

FIND IT

PAIR WORK **Student A: Think of an event that is happening in your town or city. You can also use your phone to find an event. Then invite your partner. Student B: Say no at first. Then change your mind.**

4.4 WAITING FOR SOMETHING SPECIAL

LESSON OBJECTIVE
- write an online event announcement

1 LISTENING

Congress Avenue Bridge Austin, Texas

rock concert

bats

Batman

A PREDICT **Look at the pictures from an unusual event. Can you guess what it is?**

B 1.44 **Listen to a news report about the event. Was your prediction correct?**

C 1.44 LISTEN FOR DETAIL **Listen to the report again and answer the questions.**

1 Where does the festival take place?
2 Where do the bats come from?
3 What moment are the people waiting for?
4 How many bats are there?

D 1.45 PAIR WORK **What other things do you think happen at the festival? Think of four to six possibilities. Listen and check your ideas.**

E THINK CRITICALLY **Not everyone in Austin likes the festival. Think of who these people are. Why don't they enjoy it? Would you like to go to the festival? Why or why not?**

2 PRONUNCIATION: Listening for single sounds

A 1.46 **Listen. Focus on the letters in bold. Can you hear one or two sounds?**

1 We know them from ba**d d**reams.
2 Bats a**r**e **r**eally scary.
3 There'**s s**o much happening.

B 1.47 **Find two letters in the sentences that can connect to make one sound. There are two pairs of letters in sentence 1. Listen and check.**

1 They can eat ten thousand kilograms of insects in one night.
2 It's home to music festivals and car racing.
3 I can't wait to try the barbecue.

C **Complete the sentence.**

Two sounds often become *one* / *three* if they are *similar* / *different* at the end of a word and the start of the next word.

3 WRITING

A Read the online event announcement for another unusual festival. Would you like to go to Bug Fest? Why or why not?

BugFest

September 19, 1:00 p.m.
City Museum of Science

Welcome to Bug Fest!

A celebration of the wonderful world of insects! Come and join us on the 19th and find out why we love bugs. There's something for everyone!

- ***All day***
  Scientists from the museum are presenting their favorite bugs.
- ***12:00–3:00 p.m.***
  Our team of top chefs is also cooking some great insect dishes.
- ***10:00 a.m.–1:00 p.m.***
  Two local artists are painting the bugs. You can paint them, too.
- ***1:00 p.m.–late***
  We have music as well! Local bands are playing in the museum gardens.

B **WRITING SKILLS** Find the words *also*, *as well*, and *too* in the announcement. What do they all mean?

a in addition **b** to finish

C Look at the announcement again. Check (✓) the information you can see.

activities ☐ address ☐ date ☐ place ☐ price ☐ time ☐

WRITE IT

D Write an event announcement. Follow the instructions in the form.

Add the name of your event here.

Add the time and/or date here.

Add the location here.

Add a short description here (max 30 words).

E **GROUP WORK** Look at your group's event announcements. Write a short comment on each one saying that you will go or explaining why you can't. If you decide to go, say what interests you about each event.

4.5

TIME TO SPEAK
The gift of giving

LESSON OBJECTIVE
- choose gifts for your host

A **Think about these questions:**

- When you travel to another city or country, what gifts do you bring back for your friends and family?
- What kinds of things do you like to receive as gifts?
- Look at the gift ideas on the right. Are they good to choose for your family and friends?
- What other gifts do you prefer to give them?

B **DISCUSS** **Imagine you are going to stay with a friend in another country next week. You are going to give your host two gifts: (a) something typical from your town or region and (b) something funny. You can only spend $50. Consider the following things.**

- How are you traveling? (Plane? Train?)
- Is your host male or female?
- Is your host old or young?

C **PRESENT** **Tell the class about your gifts. Explain why you made these choices and how much you're going to spend.**

D **AGREE** **Which gifts are (a) unusual or interesting, and (b) very typical of your region? Choose the two gifts to give your host.**

To check your progress, go to page 154.

USEFUL PHRASES

DISCUSS
What do you think of … ?
What's a typical gift from our town?
I love this gift because …

PRESENT
We're buying … because …
We're spending $20 on …

AGREE
I think so, too.
Good idea.
I like that idea a lot.

UNIT OBJECTIVES

- talk about past events in your life
- ask questions about the past
- congratulate and sympathize with people
- write a comment agreeing or disagreeing with an online post
- summarize a story

FIRSTS AND LASTS

5

START SPEAKING

A Look at the picture. Where are the children? What are they doing for the first time? Are they all happy? Why or why not?

B Think of a special picture of you as a child. What are you doing in the picture? Where are you? Is anyone else there? For ideas, watch Allison's video.

REAL STUDENT

Is your picture different from Allison's?

5.1 ONE AMAZING DAY

LESSON OBJECTIVE

- talk about past events in your life

1 LANGUAGE IN CONTEXT

A **Look at the photos below. What are the people doing for the first time? Are their experiences positive or negative? Why do you think so? Read their stories. Were your answers correct?**

GLOSSARY

run a red light (*v*) drive through a red traffic light

marathon (*n*) a running race of 26 miles (42 kilometers)

B **Complete the sentences with the names *Carol*, *Malik*, or *Barbara*. Whose story do you find most interesting? Why?**

1 ____________ describes an accident.

2 ____________ talks about a competition.

3 ____________ talks about a birthday.

4 ____________ says where he/she lives.

2 VOCABULARY: Describing opinions and feelings

A 1.48 **Match the four adjectives in the box with the correct emojis below. Then find and underline eight more adjectives in the stories on page 44. Match them with the other emojis. Listen and check.**

~~cool~~ crazy loud strange

1 cool P

2

3

4

5

6

7

8

9

10

11

12

B **Decide if each adjective is generally positive (*P*), negative (*N*), or can be both (*B*).**

C **Now do the vocabulary exercises for 5.1 on page 145.**

D PAIR WORK **Look at the words in the box. Use the words from exercise 2A to describe them.**

bike-sharing programs	birthdays	concerts	fast cars
festivals	my street	soccer	video games

Bike sharing programs are fun.

I don't know. I think biking in the city is dangerous.

3 GRAMMAR: Simple past

A **Complete the rules below. Use the sentences in the grammar box to help you.**

1 The simple past of *be* is ______ or *were*. The negative is *wasn't* or ______.

2 The simple past of regular verbs ends in *-ed*. For example, ______.

3 The simple past of irregular verbs doesn't end in *-ed*. For example, ______.

Simple past

I **visited** the ocean for the first time in my life.
I **ran** a red light and **hit** another car.

It **was** my first marathon.
My friends **weren't** with me.

B **Now go to page 133. Look at the grammar chart and do the grammar exercise for 5.1.**

C **Marina is talking about her first love. Complete the text with the simple past of the verbs in the box.**

be go live move not be talk

I remember my first love very well. His name [1] ______ Raúl. We [2] ______ on the same street, and we [3] ______ to the same school. He was funny, and he always [4] ______ about cool and interesting things. We [5] ______ together for a long time because his family [6] ______ to another city, but I have very nice memories of him.

D PAIR WORK **Think about an important person in your life when you were younger. Tell your partner about this person. Use the simple past.**

4 SPEAKING

PAIR WORK **Think of a special day in your life. Where were you? Who was with you? What happened? Was it a good or a bad experience? Tell your partner.**

5.2 GUESS IN 60 SECONDS

LESSON OBJECTIVE
- ask questions about the past

1 VOCABULARY: Describing life events

A 1.49 **Listen and say the life events. Write five of them under the pictures.**

be born	buy a house or apartment	graduate from college	get married
get a job	become a grandparent	have a baby	retire (stop working)
buy a car	meet your future wife/husband	learn to drive	start school

A 

B 

C 

D 

E 

B PAIR WORK **Write the 12 life events in the order that they usually happen. Compare with a partner. Are they in the same order? Explain your choices.**

C **Now do the vocabulary exercises for 5.2 on page 145.**

2 LANGUAGE IN CONTEXT

A 1.50 **Look at the pictures. Can you guess the famous man? Listen to Carla try to guess. Number the pictures in the order you hear them.**

1.50 Audio script

Carla Was he **born** in 1954?
Host Yes, he was.
Carla And did he die in 1989?
Host No, he didn't. He died in 2011.
Carla Hmm, when did he retire?
Host He **retired** in 1989.
Carla OK! Umm. Did he study medicine?
Host Yes, he did.
Carla OK. The "six." That's difficult. I don't know. Did he **get married** six times?
Host No, he didn't.
Carla Did he **buy** six **cars**?
Host No, he didn't. Think about family …
Carla Children! How many children did he have?
Host He had six children. Correct! You have ten seconds.
Carla Did he come from Argentina?
Host No, he didn't come from Argentina.
Carla Did he come from Brazil?
Host Yes, he did!
Carla OK. Sports. Was he an athlete?
Host Yes, but what was the sport? And we're out of time. Carla, for $1,000, who is the famous person?

B Write six sentences about the famous person in exercise 2A.

He was born in 1954.

C 1.51 Who is the famous person? Listen and check. Were you right?

3 GRAMMAR: Simple past negative and questions

A Complete the rules. Use the sentences in the grammar box to help you.

1 Use ______________ when you ask a question.

2 Use ______________ to make a negative.

3 The main verb in questions and negatives **is / isn't** in the simple past.

Simple past negative and questions

Did he **die** in 1989?	No, he **didn't**. He died in 2011.
Did he **come** from Argentina?	He **didn't come** from Argentina.

B 1.52 Look at these verbs from exercise 1A on page 46. Write the correct simple past form. Listen and say the words.

1 get ______	3 become ______	5 meet ______
2 have ______	4 buy ______	

C Now go to page 134. Look at the grammar chart and do the grammar exercise for 5.2.

D PAIR WORK Correct these false statements about the famous person using the simple past negative. Then check your accuracy.

1 He had seven children.

2 He studied French.

3 He came from Mexico.

4 He became a soccer player in 1954.

5 He died in 1989.

He didn't have seven children. He had six children.

ACCURACY CHECK

Don't use the simple past after *did* or *didn't* in questions and negatives.

I didn't ~~studied~~ last night. ✗

I didn't study last night. ✓

4 SPEAKING

PAIR WORK Draw six small pictures about what you did last weekend. Ask your partner questions about their pictures. Ask for extra information. For ideas, watch Irene's video.

Did you go for coffee last weekend?

Yes, I did.

Where did you go?

REAL STUDENT

Did you do the same things last weekend as Irene?

5.3 THAT'S COOL!

LESSON OBJECTIVE
- congratulate and sympathize with people

A

B

1 FUNCTIONAL LANGUAGE

A 1.53 **Look at the pictures. What do you think is happening? What are they saying to each other? Read and listen to the conversations. Were you right?**

1.53 Audio script

1
A Hey, I made it!! What a fantastic experience!
B **Congratulations**, Johnny! **Great job**!
A It was really scary at the top!
B You're right, it wasn't easy, and the weather was terrible.
A Not bad for my first time, huh?
B **You did really well**. I'm proud of you.
A You know what? Now, I want to climb another mountain.
B **That's great news**! Let's do it!

2
A Oh, no! I failed my chemistry final.
B **I'm so sorry**, Ana.
A I failed by two points!
B **That's terrible! Talk about bad luck.**
A I know, right? Oh, I can't believe this!
B **Never mind**. You can take the class again over the summer.
A Really?
B Yes, **don't worry about it**, Ana. **It's not the end of the world.**

B **Complete the chart with expressions in bold from the conversations above.**

Congratulations (good news)	Sympathy (bad news)
Congratulations!	I'm so [4] ______.
[1] ______ job!	That's terrible! Talk about [5] ______.
You did [2] ______!	[6] ______ mind.
That's [3] ______ news!	Don't worry about it. It's not [7] ______.

C PAIR WORK **Practice the conversations in exercise 1A with a partner. Then change the good and bad news and practice again.**

2 REAL-WORLD STRATEGY

A 1.54 **Listen to a short conversation. What test did the person take? What information does the person get wrong?**

CHECKING YOUR UNDERSTANDING

When you want to check your understanding of what someone said, you can ask a question with *mean*.

You mean ... ? *So, you mean ... .*

Do you mean ... ? *I thought you said ... .*

The reply often includes the phrase, *I meant ... .*

B 1.55 **Read the information in the box above about checking your understanding. Then complete another short conversation with one of the questions from the box. Listen and check.**

A Well, I failed my driver's test.
B Oh, I'm so sorry.
A Why? It's amazing! I can finally drive!
B But ____________ you *failed* the test?
A No! Ha! I meant "passed," not "failed." Duh! I passed my driver's test. I'm just so excited!!

C PAIR WORK **Student A go to page 157. Student B go to page 159. Follow the instructions.**

3 PRONUNCIATION: Saying the stress in words

A 1.56 **Listen to the words. How many syllables do you hear in each word?**

1 amazing 3
2 sorry ____
3 congratulations ____
4 terrible ____
5 impressed ____
6 fantastic ____

B 1.57 **Listen. Which speaker, A or B, uses word stress clearly?**

	A	B
1 amazing	☐	☐
2 congratulations	☐	☐
3 fantastic	☐	☐
4 horrible	☐	☐
5 terrible	☐	☐

C GROUP WORK **Practice the conversations below. Take turns being A, B, and C. Focus on word stress.**

1 **A** I passed my driving test.
B That's amazing!
C You did really well.

2 **A** I got the job!
B Congratulations!
C That's fantastic!

3 **A** How was the test?
B I failed. It was horrible!
C Yes, it was terrible! I failed, too.

4 SPEAKING

PAIR WORK **Read the situations. Practice responding to the news with your partner.**

1 Your old friend tells you that he or she got married recently. Congratulate him/her on the news.
2 A coworker of yours didn't get the job he/she really wanted. Sympathize and try to make him/her feel better.
3 Your neighbors' daughter just found out that she is going to a very good university. Congratulate her.
4 Your favorite teacher was in a car accident. He isn't hurt, but his car is totally dead. He loved that car. Sympathize with him.

5.4 FIRST IMPRESSIONS

LESSON OBJECTIVE

- write a comment agreeing or disagreeing with an online post

1 READING

A PAIR WORK Look at the pictures. Which picture is Chicago? Which is Bristol? Which is Melbourne?

B READ FOR MAIN IDEAS Read the posts. What kind of website is this? Who is positive, and who is negative about their first day?

A

A stranger in a strange town

Rafael: I went to Chicago about ten years ago for a work project. I remember the moment I stepped off the bus from the airport. Everything was strange – the smells, the crowds, the language – and everyone was in a hurry. The weather was also very cold. I needed warm clothes, and fast! In Mexico, we don't have winters like that!

B

Julia: I'm from Cologne in Germany. At age 20 I went to the U.K. as an exchange student. I remember my first day at the university in Bristol. It was scary, but then I looked around and saw so many other people in my situation. I thought, "They must feel the same." That helped. And it was a beautiful September day. Suddenly, I felt so positive.

C

Kamal: I was born in Nepal, but I went to live in Melbourne, Australia, as an immigrant worker. On that first day, I didn't understand any English, but I remember that people were friendly. I smiled, and they smiled back. I walked along the river and felt very free. Everything was clean and new, like a fresh start.

Send your first impressions to 1stday@ourplanet.com

C READ FOR DETAILS Read the posts again. Check (✓) the sentences that are true. Correct the false ones.

- [ ] 1 Rafael was prepared for his arrival in Chicago.
- [ ] 2 The weather is different in Rafael's country.
- [ ] 3 Julia went to Bristol for work.
- [ ] 4 Julia felt very scared and alone, and those feelings never changed.
- [ ] 5 When he arrived, Kamal already knew some English.
- [ ] 6 For Kamal, his first day was like a new beginning.

D PAIR WORK THINK CRITICALLY Imagine what these people say about your hometown. Do they say the same things or different things?

- an exchange student from another country
- a businessperson
- an immigrant worker

2 WRITING

A **Look at these comments on the posts in exercise 1B. Match them to the correct posts. Write *R* (Rafael), *J* (Julia), or *K* (Kamal).**

Tweets   Tweets & replies   Media

___ 1 **@tobytwo: I know the feeling**, I didn't understand a word of English on my first day. It was just terrible!

___ 2 **@TheresaB: Interesting, but** my first days in the U.K. weren't like that. It rained and rained. 😊

___ 3 **@cigdemyilmaz4: No way!** I didn't like being an exchange student at all. I missed my home all the time. Didn't you miss it?

___ 4 **@patricianuñez12: Are you kidding?** So what if the weather isn't the best? It's a great town! Buy a coat and keep an open mind.

___ 5 **@daviddaly: Absolutely!** 🙄 My first day in San Diego was the same – all those people, all those strange sounds and smells – it was amazing, actually!

___ 6 **@titusx2: You're so right.** I hated Canada when I arrived – so cold and unfriendly – but I call it home now. Don't trust your first ideas about something!

B **Which of the six comments agree with the posts? Which disagree?**

C WRITING SKILLS **Look at the expressions in bold in the comments. Are they to agree or disagree?**

Agree: *I know the feeling,* ______________, ______________

Disagree: *Interesting, but ...,* ______________, ______________

WRITE IT

D **Write a comment to Rafael, Julia, or Kamal agreeing or disagreeing with their posts. Use the expressions in exercise 2C. Why do you agree or disagree? What information should you include?**

REGISTER CHECK

You can say *Are you crazy?*, *Seriously?*, *Are you kidding?* when the person is a friend or someone you know well.

5.5 TIME TO SPEAK
Iceberg!

LESSON OBJECTIVE
- summarize a story

The Titanic left Southampton, England, for New York on April 10, 1912. It was the ship's first time at sea.

The Titanic hit an iceberg off the coast of Canada on April 14. It made a hole, and the ship started to sink very quickly.

Some passengers and crew escaped on lifeboats. Survivors were rescued by another ship, the Carpathia, on April 15.

FIND IT

A **RESEARCH** Look at the pictures and read the captions. What do you know about the story of the Titanic? If you can, go online to see more pictures and learn the full story of the famous accident.

B **PREPARE** You are going to read a story about a person who was on the Titanic. Divide into four groups (A, B, C, and D) and follow the instructions for your group. Then answer the questions below and take notes.

Group A: Go to page 157.
Group B: Go to page 158.
Group C: Go to page 159.
Group D: Go to page 160.

1 How old was the person?
2 Where was the person from?
3 Was the person a passenger or a crew member? If a passenger, what type of ticket did the person have?
4 Did the person survive? If so, how?
5 What did the person do in the years after the accident?

C **PRESENT** Make new groups with one person each from groups A, B, C, and D. Tell your new group about your person using your notes. Take notes on the other stories that you hear.

We read about Carla Jensen. She was from Denmark and was only 19. She traveled …

D **DISCUSS** Discuss all the people in your stories. What do they all have in common? How are they different? Whose story do you like most? Why?

Carla traveled third class. She didn't have much money, but Molly was rich …

To check your progress, go to page 154.

USEFUL PHRASES

RESEARCH
The picture shows …
What does it say about … ?
I can't find the answer. Where does it tell you about … ?

PRESENT
Our group read about …
After that … / Then … / Later …

DISCUSS
They all traveled/survived/worked …
I thought his/her story was really sad/inspiring/interesting.
I liked this story most because …

UNIT OBJECTIVES

- plan a shopping trip
- talk about shopping habits
- describe what you want in a store
- write a script for a vlog
- present an idea for a new invention

BUY NOW, PAY LATER

6

START SPEAKING

A Look at the picture. Where are the people? What are they doing?

B How often do you go shopping? What type of things do you usually buy?

C Is there a market like the one in the picture where you live? Do you shop there? What other places do you go shopping? For ideas, watch Irene's video.

Do you agree with Irene?

6.1 BLACK FRIDAY FUN

LESSON OBJECTIVE
- plan a shopping trip

1 LANGUAGE IN CONTEXT

FIND IT

A 1.58 PAIR WORK **What do you know about Black Friday? You can go online to find out more. Then listen to four people talking about Black Friday. Who likes the day?**

B 1.58 **Listen to the program again. Who ... ?**

1 ______________ wants a new television.
2 ______________ works at the store.
3 ______________ is with someone.
4 ______________ made a mistake.

1.58 Audio script

Black Friday is back! We asked some people what they think of it. Here's what they said.

Katie I didn't know today was Black Friday. I only came here to **return** a shirt but forget it! I'm going to come back next week – when it's not so crazy!

Seb I love Black Friday. I **save** for months and months and even **borrow** money from friends. I go crazy! I usually **spend** my money on clothes and shoes, but this year I'm going to buy a TV.

Marcia I hate Black Friday! I have to work all day and, excuse me. . . . Are you going to buy that?

Adam I'm here with my wife, but I can't find her now! I really want to go home. We're not going to come back next year. We're going to **shop online** in the future.

C PAIR WORK **Do you think Black Friday is a good idea? Why or why not?**

2 VOCABULARY: Using money

A 1.59 **Listen and say the words. Then match the words to the correct definition.**

borrow ☐	cost ☐	lend ☐	pay back ☐	return ☐
save ☐	sell ☐	shop online 1	spend ☐	waste ☐

1 buy things on the internet
2 give something to people for money
3 keep money for the future
4 use something that belongs to someone for a short time
5 not use money in a good way
6 have a price
7 give something to someone for a time
8 use money to pay for something
9 give someone the money that they gave you
10 take something back to the store because you don't like it or it isn't right

B **Now do the vocabulary exercises for 6.1 on page 146.**

C PAIR WORK **Do you waste money on things you don't need? For ideas, watch Allison's video.**

! We can *spend time* or *waste time*.
I like to ***spend time*** *with my friends.*
Don't ***waste your time*** *on video games.*

REAL STUDENT

Are you the same as Allison?

3 GRAMMAR: *be going to*

A **Answer the questions. Use the sentences in the grammar box to help you.**

1 Does *going to* describe an action in the past, present, or future? ______

2 When you use *going to*, are you sure about your plans or not? ______

be going to

This year I**'m going to** buy a TV.	**Are** you **going to** buy that?
We**'re going to** shop online in the future.	We**'re not going to** come back next year.

B **Now go to page 134. Look at the grammar chart and do the grammar exercise for 6.1.**

C PAIR WORK **What are <u>you</u> going to do this month? Write four sentences about your plans. Then check your accuracy.**

free time	friends and family	home
study	work	

✓ ACCURACY CHECK

When you talk about future plans, remember to use the *-ing* form of *go*.

I ~~go~~ to sell my house. ✗

I'm going to sell my house. ✓

D PAIR WORK **Tell your partner about your plans. Then tell another pair of students about your partner's plans.**

I'm going to start my new job on Monday.

Paolo is going to start his new job next week.

4 SPEAKING

A PAIR WORK **Read the ad. Plan a Black Friday shopping trip. Use the words and phrases to help you.**

- When / go?
- What / buy?
- How long / stay there?
- How much / spend?

When are we going to go?

B **Tell the class about your plans.**

We're going to go shopping on Friday morning before they sell everything. We're going to buy a flat-screen TV. We're not going to spend over $200.

6.2 SHOP THIS WAY

LESSON OBJECTIVE
- talk about shopping habits

1 VOCABULARY: Shopping

A 1.60 PAIR WORK **Listen and say the words. Then, with a partner, find the words in the pictures. Write a number in each box. Can you find all of them?**

[1] (shopping) cart	[ ] cash register	[ ] checkout	[ ] customers	[ ] department store
[ ] grocery store	[ ] price	[ ] sale	[ ] salesperson	[ ] shelf

B **Now do the vocabulary exercises for 6.2 on page 146.**

C PAIR WORK **Make notes about a recent shopping trip. How many words from exercise 1A can you use? Tell your partner about it.**

2 LANGUAGE IN CONTEXT

A PAIR WORK **Think of a time you bought something you didn't need. Why did you buy it?**

B **Read the blog post. Find three things that stores do to make us buy more things.**

*Never go to the **grocery store** when you're hungry!*

I go grocery shopping most weekends, but I don't like it. I go early, and I don't waste time. But today I went after work to get some eggs for dinner. Big mistake!

When I walked in, I turned right, as most people do. Stores always put their sale items to the right. I put some cheese and some meat in my **cart** because they were on sale. Then I saw the desserts. All of them were on the middle **shelf**. Did you know that stores put expensive things on the middle shelf because that's where customers look first? I put two desserts into my cart. Then I smelled the bread. Stores know that fresh bread makes people hungry. Yep, I bought bread, too. I now had many items in my cart! On the way to the **checkout**, I counted 12 things but no eggs. EGGS! I almost forgot. I went to the egg shelf, but there were none left!

C PAIR WORK **What are your shopping habits? Tell your partner.**

3 GRAMMAR: Determiners

A **Circle the correct options to complete the rules. Use the sentences in the grammar box to help you.**

1 After determiners like *no*, *some*, and *many*, we use a **singular / plural** noun. This is when we want to talk about **specific things / things in general**.

2 We use a determiner + *of* + *the* + plural noun/object pronoun (*you, us, them*) when we want to talk about **specific things / things in general**.

Determiners

I go grocery shopping **most** weekends.	I now had **many** items in my cart.
I went after work to get **some** eggs for dinner.	I counted 12 things, but **no** eggs.
All of them were on the middle shelf.	There were **none** left.

B **Look at the bold words in the box above. Write them in the correct order below.**

none/no ➡ ________ ➡ ________ ➡ ________ ➡ ________

0% … 100%

C **Now go to page 135. Look at the grammar chart and do the grammar exercise for 6.2.**

D PAIR WORK **Write sentences about the stores in your town. Use *all*, *most*, *many*, *some*, *none*, or *no*. Tell your partner. Do you both agree?**

> **!** ***no* or *none*?**
> ***no** customers*
> ***none of the** customers*

4 SPEAKING

A GROUP WORK **Look at the customer survey. Ask your classmates the questions and make notes about their answers.**

B **Share what you learned in exercise 4A.**

Most of the students in this class …

Some of us … .

None of us … .

HELP US **HELP YOU**

We want to know about our customers.

- Do you prefer shopping with a friend or alone? Why?
- Do you always wait for things to go on sale? Why or why not?
- What's your favorite place to go shopping? Why?
- What is one thing you don't like about shopping? Why?

6.3 WHAT DO YOU CALL THEM IN ENGLISH?

LESSON OBJECTIVE
- describe what you want in a store

A 

B 

1 FUNCTIONAL LANGUAGE

INSIDER ENGLISH

Use *get* as another way to say *I understand*.

A **Look at the pictures. What type of store are the two customers in?**

B 1.61 **Read and listen to the two conversations. What do the two people buy? Match each conversation to a picture.**

1.61 Audio script

1 A Hi, how can I help you?
B Hello. I'm looking for some things. **You cut your nails with them.**
A What? Oh, you mean "scissors"?
B No. **They're like** scissors, but they're just for nails.
A Oh, got it. Yes, we have them. Nail clippers.
B **What do you call them in English**?
A Nail clippers.

2 A Hi there. Can I help you?
B Hello. I'm looking for … um … **I don't know the word** in English. **It's a thing for** my phone.
A A cable?
B No. **You use it to** connect the power cord to the electricity when you're in another country.
A Mm … Oh, I get it! There's one over there. That works for all countries.
B Thanks. **How do you say that in English**?
A It's an adapter. A universal adapter.

C **Complete the chart with expressions in bold from the conversations above.**

Explaining your language problem	Explaining the function of the thing you want
I don't know [1] ______ in English.	[2] ______ (cut your nails) [3] ______ it/them. [4] ______ ______ it/them [5] ______ (connect the power cord). They're/It's [6] ______ (scissors), but … . It's [7] ______ ______ ______ (my phone).

D PAIR WORK **Practice the conversations in exercise 1B with your partner.**

2 REAL-WORLD STRATEGY

ASKING FOR WORDS IN ENGLISH

When you want to know a new word, you can ask how to say it in English.

What do you call it/them in English?

How do you say that in English?

What's the English word for … ?

A 1.62 **Read about how to ask for words in English in the box above. Then listen to another conversation in a shop. What does the person buy? Which question from the box does he use?**

B 1.63 **Read the short conversation. What do you call it in English? Listen and check.**

A You use it at the supermarket to carry the things you want to buy.

B Oh, yeah, got it. It's a thing for your groceries. You push it. But what do you call it in English?

A It's a …

FIND IT

C PAIR WORK **Find three things in the classroom or in your bag that you don't know how to say in English. Use a dictionary or your phone to find the words in English. Have short conversations with your partner like the one in exercise 2B.**

3 PRONUNCIATION: Stressing important words

A 1.64 **Listen to the conversation. Notice that important words (usually nouns, verbs, adjectives, or adverbs) are stressed (they're louder and clearer).**

A What? Oh, you mean scissors?

B No. They're like scissors, but they're just for nails.

B 1.65 **Underline the important words in the conversation below. Then listen. Do the speakers stress the words you underlined? Practice saying the sentences.**

A I'm looking for something for my phone.

B A phone charger?

A No. You use it to connect your phone to electricity.

B A power cord!

4 SPEAKING

PAIR WORK **Student A: Go to page 158. Student B: Go to page 160. Follow the instructions.**

6.4 MONEY LESSONS

LESSON OBJECTIVE
- write a script for a vlog

1 LISTENING

A PAIR WORK **Think of someone you know who gives good money advice. What advice does he/she give you? Tell a partner.**

B PREDICT **You're going to listen to three stories about problems with money. Look at the pictures. Where do the three stories happen?**

A ☐

B ☐
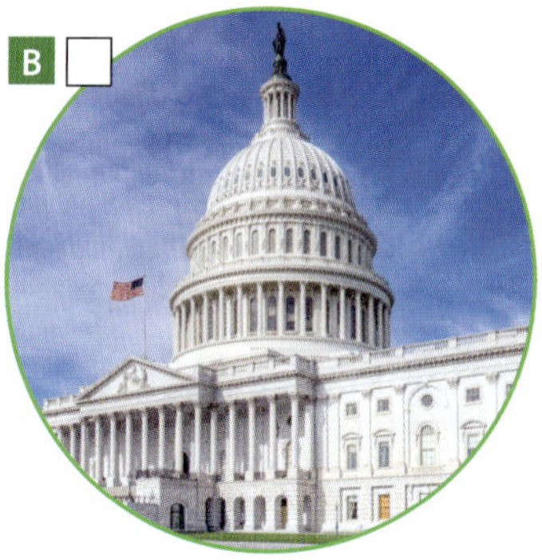

C ☐

C 1.66 **Listen to the stories. Match the stories (1–3) to the pictures (A–C). Were your answers in exercise 1B correct?**

D 1.66 LISTEN FOR DETAIL **Listen to the podcast again. Check (✓) the sentences that are true. Correct the false ones.**

___ 1 The women spent many hours drinking tea.
___ 2 The women borrowed some money from a man in the café.
___ 3 Rosa had $60 in her bag when she was in the taxi.
___ 4 The money was still in her bag when she got it back.
___ 5 Senator Richard Burr didn't want people to see him enter his PIN.
___ 6 The Senator left his cash in the ATM.

E THINK CRITICALLY PAIR WORK **Look at the three money lessons the speakers learned. Which lesson do you agree most with? Explain your answer.**

- Some things are more important than money.
- Pay attention when you're at the ATM.
- When you travel, check that the banks are open.

2 PRONUNCIATION: Listening for weak words

A 1.67 **Listen to the sentences from the stories. Circle the words that aren't stressed.**

It was the long New Year's weekend a couple of years ago.
None of their ATM cards worked in Japan.

B 1.68 PAIR WORK **Listen and write in the missing words. Compare with a partner.**

1 What did you ______________ the movie last night?
2 I'm all ______________ cash.

C **Complete the sentence.**

A weak form of the word ______________ is often used when it's between other words.

3 WRITING

A **Read the advice website on how to save money. How many of the suggestions do you agree with?**

Top tips to save money
– spending less on the little things in life.

1. One in, one out. When you buy a new shirt, sell or give away an old **one**.
2. Going to the movies? Don't buy snacks at the theater. Go to a store to buy **them** before you go.
3. A "2-for-1" deal isn't always a *good* deal. When a store offers two big bags of chips for $5.00, and a single bag is $3.00, you save $1.00, and that's great! Or is it? If you didn't need all those chips, then you paid $2.00 for something that you didn't really want.
4. Better to borrow than buy. If you only need to wear something once – for example, a suit for a job interview – ask a friend to lend you one.
5. Don't join a gym! If you're going to exercise just once a week, don't waste money on an annual subscription. It's usually cheaper to pay for each fitness class.
6. Go grocery shopping in the evening. That's when supermarkets have sales on many items, and you can fill your cart with more for less!

GLOSSARY
give away (*v*) give something to someone and not ask for money
snack (*n*) a small amount of food between meals
subscription (*n*) money that you pay regularly for a service

B **With a partner, decide if the suggestions in exercise 3A are about clothes (C), free time (FT), or shopping (S). Then add two more suggestions for each one.**

C WRITING SKILLS **Look at the words in bold in the website. Underline the word in each sentence that *one* and *them* refer to. Find the other example of *one* in the website and underline the word it refers to.**

D **Rewrite the sentences with the words in parentheses ( ).**

1 If you want a new sweater, you can probably find a new sweater in the sale section for less than full price. (one)

2 If you have some pants or a shirt that you didn't wear last year, you're probably not going to wear the pants or shirt this year, either. (them)

WRITE IT

E **Imagine you have a vlog. In today's vlog, you are going to make suggestions for saving money on the two topics below. Write your script. Don't forget to use *one* and *them* when you can.**

phone transportation

F **Work with a partner and film your vlog. Watch the vlogs in class and say what the best advice is.**

6.5 TIME TO SPEAK
Eureka!

LESSON OBJECTIVE
- present an idea for a new invention

folding bicycle

banana protector

cardboard VR headset (VR = Virtual Reality)

longboard baby stroller

A **Look at the ideas in the photos with a partner. What are they for? Why are they useful?**

B **The best ideas help solve a problem. With a partner, match the ideas in exercise A with the problems they help solve.**

1 VR headsets are very expensive. ___
2 My bicycle is too big to fit on the bus or train. ___
3 Bananas become soft and brown in my bag. ___
4 Baby strollers are heavy and slow. ___

C **DISCUSS** **Here are more problems. Think of an idea to help solve them. Be creative! Use the phrases at the bottom of the page to help you.**

- I often forget where I put my phone.
- Grocery bags full of food are really heavy, and they sometimes break.
- I hate my alarm clock. It's so loud, and I wake up tired and unhappy.
- My dog needs more exercise, but I don't have time in the evenings for a walk.
- I need somewhere to put my cold drink when I'm at the beach.

INVENTORS WANTED!

Do you have an **amazing idea** for a **new invention**? We want to buy it!

Tell us about your idea. We want to know:

- what are you going to call your invention?
- how is it going to work?
- what problem is it going to solve?
- how much is it going to cost?
- who is going to buy it?

D **PREPARE** **Read the announcement above. You are going to present one of your ideas from exercise C. Discuss the questions in the announcement to help you prepare your presentation.**

E **PRESENT** **Present your invention to the class. Listen to the other presentations and ask questions about their ideas.**

F **Imagine you and your group are business experts. You have $5,000. You can give this all to one group, or share it between different groups. Talk about the ideas you thought were good. Who are you going to give the money to, and why?**

To check your progress, go to page 154.

USEFUL PHRASES

DISCUSS
Maybe a … / What about a …
… would be useful.
I have an idea for a …
That sounds great!
I love that idea!

PREPARE
My favorite idea was …
Who's going to talk about … ?

PRESENT
We're going to tell you about our new idea …
People are going to love it because …
It's really simple/useful/ fun.
We think it's going to make lots of money.

REVIEW 2 (UNITS 4–6)

1 VOCABULARY

A Look at the word cloud. Find five words or phrases for each category below.

fun candle department store musician amazing grocery store borrow graduate from college retire bouquet of flowers candy perfume artist get married jewelry crazy have a baby buy a house cool actor cost shelf checkout singer spend save sale strange director lend

1 pop culture: *actor,* __________

2 gifts: __________

3 opinions: __________

4 life events: __________

5 using money: __________

6 shopping: __________

B Add three more words or phrases that you know to each category.

2 GRAMMAR

A Complete the sentences with the present continuous or simple past of the verbs in parentheses ( ). Then find the object pronouns (*you*, *me*, *us*, etc.) and circle them. What nouns do they replace? Underline them.

1 My father __________ (retire) next week. His coworkers __________ (plan) a party for him.

2 My best friend __________ (start) her new job last Monday.

3 My sister __________ (get) married next Saturday. We're all very excited!

4 Yesterday __________ (be) my neighbor's 75th birthday. I __________ (not go) to his party because I __________ (not be) home.

5 My boss and her family __________ (move) to their new house next month. We should buy her a gift.

6 My cousin and her husband __________ (have) a baby two weeks ago. I'm so happy for them.

B PAIR WORK Write five sentences about big events in your life and the lives of people you know using the present continuous and simple past. Read your sentences with a partner.

C Look at the sentences you wrote in 2B again. Are your object pronouns correct? Underline the nouns that your object pronouns replace to check. Correct your work.

3 SPEAKING

PAIR WORK You need to buy a gift for each of the people in Grammar exercise 2A. Answer the questions.

- What are you going to buy?
- Where are you going to buy it?
- How much are you going to spend?

I'm going to buy my grandfather a book about boats. He loves boats. I'm going to buy it online. I'm not going to spend more than $30.

4 FUNCTIONAL LANGUAGE

A Use the words and phrases in the box to complete the conversation.

congratulations	I can't	love to	meet
sorry to hear	too bad	we're going	would you like

A Hey, guess what? I got the job!

B Wow, that's great! [1] ______________ !

A Thanks! [2] ______________ to come out and celebrate with us? [3] ______________ bowling and then getting pizza.

B I'd really [4] ______________ , but [5] ______________ . I failed one of my tests last week, and I need to take it again on Monday. So I'm studying the whole weekend.

A Oh no, that's [6] ______________ . I'm really [7] ______________ that. Maybe you could only come out for pizza, then. Just for an hour? Come on! You need to eat.

B Oh, OK. Where are you going?

A Great! Let's [8] ______________ at Dom's Pizza at eight. See you there!

B Read the sentences. Can you guess what it is?

1 I'm looking for a bag to hold money and other things. I don't know the word in English.

2 I'm looking for a thing for my phone, for the battery. I don't know how to say it in English.

3 I don't know the word in English, but it's something for my groceries. I mean, you use it to put food in when you go around the grocery store.

5 SPEAKING

A PAIR WORK **Choose one of the situations below. Act it out in pairs.**

1 Imagine it's your birthday tomorrow. Decide what you're going to do, where you're going to go, and when. Call a friend to ask them to come to your party.

A Hey, tomorrow's my birthday, and I'm …

B Oh, I wish I could …

2 Imagine your friend passed her driving test. Call your friend to congratulate her. Suggest doing something together to celebrate.

A I just heard that you passed your driving test!

B Yeah! I'm so excited!

3 You want to buy a gift for a friend. First decide what you want to buy. Then imagine you're in a store. Ask the clerk to help you. You don't know the word in English.

A May I help you?

B Hi, yes, I'm looking for …

B Change roles and repeat the role play.

UNIT OBJECTIVES

- talk about your favorite comfort food
- design a food truck
- explain what you want in a restaurant
- write a comment about an online article
- plan a party

EAT, DRINK, BE HAPPY

7

START SPEAKING

A Look at the picture. Who are these people? Why are they all eating together? Do you have big meals like this? When?

B In general, do you prefer eating alone or with other people? Who do you usually eat with at different meals? What do you talk about when you're eating?

C What makes a meal special: Is it the food, the people, or something else? Explain your answer. For ideas, watch Seung Geyoung's video.

REAL STUDENT

Do you agree with Seung Geyoung?

7.1 COMFORT FOOD

LESSON OBJECTIVE
- talk about your favorite comfort food

1 VOCABULARY: Naming food

A 2.02 **Look at the pictures. Which do you like? With a partner, match the food items to the words in the box. Listen and check, and then say the words.**

avocado ___	onion ___
burger ___	pasta ___
cereal ___	peanut butter 1
chili / chili pepper ___	pepper ___
corn ___	salmon ___
jam ___	salt ___
lettuce ___	strawberry ___
noodles ___	yogurt ___

B **Which food items are sweet, and which are usually not sweet? Make two lists.**

C **Now do the vocabulary exercises for 7.1 on page 147.**

2 LANGUAGE IN CONTEXT

A **What is "comfort food"? Read the blog post and find out. How many different types of chicken soup does the writer describe?**

GLOSSARY
recipe (*n*) instructions for how to prepare and cook food

A TASTE OF HOME

Everyone has their own idea of comfort food – that special dish you eat anytime you feel sad or worried.

For me, there's only one comfort food: my mom's chicken soup. Did you know that chicken soup is probably the world's favorite comfort food? It makes you feel happy, and it's quick to make – perfect when there's not much time to cook.

The classic recipe includes chicken and a little **onion**, but there are many other ways to cook it. Colombian *ajiaco* has a lot of **corn** and potatoes, in India it comes with an egg, and the Chinese serve it with **noodles** and sometimes a few **chilies**. In Korea they usually eat *samgyetang* in the summer, served with some rice.

Comfort food is very personal. It can be a full meal, a dessert, or just a snack. Tell us about *your* favorite comfort food.

B PAIR WORK **Find these words in the blog: *dessert, dish, meal, snack*. Think of an example of each one.**

C PAIR WORK **What's a famous soup in your country? Where and when do people usually eat it? You can go online to find a recipe. For ideas, watch Alessandra's video.**

FIND IT

REAL STUDENT

Would you like to try Alessandra's dish?

3 GRAMMAR: Quantifiers

A **Complete the rules. Use the pictures in the grammar box to help you. Which words can you use to talk about a large amount, a small amount, and an amount that is not large or small?**

1 Count nouns (e.g., *strawberry, avocado*) can be **only singular / only plural / singular or plural**.

2 Use *a* or ______________ with singular count nouns.

Quantifiers

Count nouns

***How many** chilies?*

a lot of chilies

some chilies

a few / not many chilies

too many chilies

Non-count nouns

***How much** rice?*

a lot of rice

some rice

a little / not much rice

too much rice

! **Some nouns can be count *and* non-count.**
You can count chili peppers (*too many chilies*) but not the small pieces we use for cooking (*too much chili*).
Think about *chicken*. When is it count, and when is it non-count?

B **Now go to page 135. Look at the grammar chart and do the grammar exercise for 7.1.**

C **Complete the questions with *much* or *many*. Then check your accuracy. Ask your partner the questions.**

1 How ___many___ cups of coffee do you drink every day?
2 How ______________ cookies do you eat in a week?
3 How ______________ yogurt do you eat at breakfast?
4 How ______________ meat or fish do you eat each week?

ACCURACY CHECK

Use *many* with plural count nouns.

There aren't ~~much~~ chilies in this dish. ✗

There aren't many chilies in this dish. ✓

4 SPEAKING

A PAIR WORK **Tell your partner about your favorite comfort food.**

> My favorite comfort food is … It's my favorite food because … I like to eat it with some / a lot of / a little …

B GROUP WORK **Ask other students about their favorite comfort food. Tell the class.**

> A lot of people like snacks and sweet food. Manuel's favorite comfort food is rice with milk and sugar.

7.2 EAT IN THE STREET

LESSON OBJECTIVE
- design a food truck

1 VOCABULARY: Describing food

A 2.03 **Listen and say the words. Now match the words to the pictures.**

bitter ~~boiled~~ delicious fresh fried grilled raw roasted sour spicy

1 
boiled

2 

3 

4 

5 

6 

7 

8 

9 

10 

B **Put the words in exercise 1A into two groups: (a) how to serve food and (b) how food tastes. One word can go in both groups. Which word?**

C **Now do the vocabulary exercises for 7.2 on page 147.**

2 LANGUAGE IN CONTEXT

A PAIR WORK **Look at the picture of a food truck. What kinds of food can you get from food trucks?**

B 2.04 **Listen to a live radio show from the Food Truck Awards. What food is Clara cooking today? Why does the customer like food trucks?**

2.04 Audio script

Host	Hi! I'm at the Food Truck Awards with one of this year's winners, Clara Montero. What are you making today, Clara?
Clara	Fish tacos! They're usually **fried**, but today the fish is **raw**. Try one! It has this great **spicy** sauce.
Host	Mm! Wow, hot! But really good. Thanks, Clara. Now, I'm sure this next truck is good because there's a long line. Hi! What are you waiting here for?
Customer	Their amazing **grilled** burgers! I usually can't stand waiting in line, but I don't mind waiting here.
Host	Yeah? Better than a restaurant?
Customer	Definitely! I prefer to eat at food trucks. They're really cool – they're cheap, you can eat outside, and the food is always **delicious**. I always want to try new food. You need to try their fries. They're amazing!
Host	Great idea, thanks. Enjoy!

INSIDER ENGLISH

hot = *spicy*

C PAIR WORK **Are there many food trucks in your town? What's your favorite dish?**

3 GRAMMAR: Verb patterns

A **Circle the correct options to complete the rules. Use the sentences in the grammar box to help you.**

1 The verb that follows verbs like *can't stand* and *don't mind* is **verb + -*ing* / *to* + verb**.

2 The verb that follows verbs like *want* and *need* is **verb + -*ing* / *to* + verb**.

Verb patterns

I usually **can't stand waiting** in line.	I always **want to try** new food.
I **don't mind waiting** here.	You **need to try** their fries.

B **Now go to page 136. Look at the grammar chart and do the grammar exercise for 7.2.**

C PAIR WORK **Choose verbs from each box and make true sentences about yourself. Tell your partner.**

can't stand, don't mind, enjoy, forget, hate, like, love, prefer, want, would like

buy, cook, eat, go out, make, shop, take

I can't stand cooking breakfast food. It's so boring!

! **Some verbs (*love, prefer, like, hate*) take both forms. The meaning doesn't change.**

I like to cook. ✓
I like cooking. ✓
I prefer to eat out. ✓
I prefer eating out. ✓

4 SPEAKING

A GROUP WORK **You are going to design your own food truck. Think about:**

- the name and look of your food truck
- what's on the menu and how it's cooked
- the prices of your food and any special deals
- who your customers are (for example, vegetarians, students)

Our food truck is called Crepe Crazy. We're going to sell all types of delicious crepes like peanut butter, cheese and onion, and strawberry. Everyone enjoys eating crepes but hates to make them at home. Our prices ....

B **Tell the class about your food truck. Which group's food truck is the best?**

7.3 I'LL HAVE THE CHICKEN

LESSON OBJECTIVE

- explain what you want in a restaurant

1 FUNCTIONAL LANGUAGE

A 2.05 **Read and listen to the conversations. What does the woman order in conversation 1? Why? In conversation 2, what's the problem with her order? In conversation 3, what does she ask for?**

2.05 Audio script

1 A Hi, **are you ready to order**?
B **What do you recommend**?
A The seafood's great here.
B But I'm allergic to seafood.
A Well, the grilled salmon is fantastic.
B I mean, I'm allergic to all seafood.
A Oh, OK. Well, the chicken is very good.
B **What does it come with**?
A It comes with French fries and a salad.
B **What kind of dressing** does it come with?
A Oil and vinegar.
B Perfect. **I'll have the** chicken, please.

2 B Excuse me – you gave me the salmon, but I ordered grilled chicken.
A I'm so sorry. I'll bring you the correct dish right away.
B Thank you.

3 A **Was everything OK for you today**?
B It was all really good, thank you.
A **Can I get you** a dessert?
B Not today, thanks. **Can I have the check**?
A Sure. Coming right up.

B **Complete the chart with expressions in bold from the conversations above.**

Ordering food	**Taking an order**
I'll 1 ________ the (chicken), please.	Are you ready 5 ________ ________ ?
	Can I 6 ________ ________ (a dessert)?
Asking questions about food	**Checking with the customer**
What do you 2 ________ ?	7 ________ ________ OK for you today?
What does it 3 ________ ________ ?	**Asking for the check**
	Can I 8 ________ the check?
What 4 ________ ________ (dressing) does it come with?	

C 2.06 PAIR WORK **Circle the correct word to complete the expressions. Listen and check. Then practice the conversations with a partner. Change the food each time.**

1 A What does the steak *go / come* with?
B Salad or fries.

2 A *How / What* was the chicken?
B Great, thanks. Can I *have / make* the check, please?

2 REAL-WORLD STRATEGY

A 2.07 **Listen to another conversation in the restaurant. What does the customer ask about the pasta?**

B 2.07 **Listen again. Why does the customer say, *I mean …* ?**

I MEAN

When you need to be clear about an order or instruction, or if you think someone doesn't really understand what you want, use *I mean* to give more detail.

Is there any meat in the pasta? I'm a vegetarian.

There's a little meat in the sauce, but not much.

I mean, I don't eat any meat.

C PAIR WORK **Read the information about *I mean* in the box above. Practice the example conversation with a partner.**

D PAIR WORK **Student A: Go to page 158. Student B: Go to page 160. Follow the instructions.**

3 PRONUNCIATION: Saying /dʒ/ and /g/ sounds

A 2.08 **Listen to the words. Focus on the sound of the letters in bold. Practice saying them.**

/dʒ/ **jet** /g/ **get**

B 2.09 **Look at the conversation. Do the bold words have the /dʒ/ sound or the /g/ sound? Listen and check. Then practice the conversation with a partner.**

A Can I **g**et you some **j**uice? We have **g**reat apple **j**uice.

B No, thanks. I'm aller**g**ic to apple **j**uice.

A **G**ot it. **J**ust some water, then?

4 SPEAKING

A PAIR WORK **Put the conversation in order. Then practice with a partner.**

[5] Sounds good. I'll have the pasta.

[ ] It's a cream and mushroom sauce.

[ ] What do you recommend? The pasta or the beef?

[ ] What kind of sauce does it have?

[ ] The pasta is delicious today.

B PAIR WORK **Choose one of the situations and have a conversation with your partner.**

- The server brings the wrong dish to a customer.
- The server doesn't understand the customer's question.
- The customer is allergic to peanuts.

7.4 IMPOSSIBLE FOODS

LESSON OBJECTIVE

- write a comment about an online article

1 READING

A **PREDICT** **Look at the picture in the article. Why do you think this is called the Impossible Burger?**

B **Read the article. Were you right? Read the article again and write the headings in the correct places.**

1 In a restaurant near you
2 Meat from plants
3 Good for the future
4 The secret ingredient

C **PAIR WORK** **THINK CRITICALLY** **Read the article again. Are Impossible Burgers the best thing to happen to food in years? Discuss the positives and negatives of green food with your partner.**

The new and wonderful world of Impossible Foods

A ______________________

Impossible Foods is a company in Silicon Valley, California. They make burgers and other delicious meat and dairy products. There's something very unusual about their food: Their meat and dairy don't come from animals, but from plants. Yes, plants! I didn't believe it at first, but it's true. Thanks to Impossible Foods, you can eat a delicious burger that looks like meat and tastes like meat but is made with only plants.

B ______________________

How does the Impossible Burger look and taste so real? The secret is something called heme. It's an ingredient that exists in both plants and animals. Heme gives raw beef its red color and meat flavor. Impossible Foods uses the heme found in plants, not animals, to make the Impossible Burger. It's healthy, and the plant ingredients don't hurt the environment. Clever, isn't it?

C ______________________

So, why is Impossible Foods doing this? Well, animal farming uses about 50% of the Earth's land and 25% of the Earth's water. That's a very expensive way to produce food. So, it seems to me that the Impossible Burger is a great example of a food of the future – good for the planet and good for your health. Soon it'll be cheap to eat, too!

D ______________________

Maybe you think all of this is science fiction, but it's not. Twenty restaurants in the U.S. now sell the Impossible Burger. Soon these delicious burgers will be everywhere. In my opinion, it's the best thing to happen to food in years!

GLOSSARY

dairy (*adj*) milk products, or food made from milk

2 WRITING

A **Look at the comments posted about the article. Who is positive, and who is negative about Impossible Foods?**

James	**I think** it's a great idea. I'm a vegetarian, but I love to eat burgers – and now I can!
Anna	I don't like to eat food that isn't natural!
Yang	Why eat a fake steak? **If you ask me**, it's like having a fake watch.
Marta	I love the idea of impossible food, but **I don't think** it's going to be popular. People prefer the real thing.
Oliver	They say it's green and cheap, but what about the cost of all the experiments? **For me**, research like this is too expensive.

B PAIR WORK **Look at the comments again. Which comments do you agree and disagree with? Why?**

C WRITING SKILLS **Look at the words in bold in the comments. Do we use these expressions to say something is true or to give an opinion?**

D **Read the Register check box. Then rewrite these sentences with a different expression than *I think*.**

1 I think Impossible Foods is a great company!

____

2 I think it's a crazy idea. I don't like food made by scientists.

____

3 I think it's good for the planet!

____

REGISTER CHECK

Here are some ways to give an opinion:

I think … If you ask me … For me …

For formal writing, like essays, use a more formal expression:

From my point of view …
It seems to me that …

WRITE IT

E **Do you think foods like the impossible burger are a good idea? Write a comment about it to post on the website.**

7.5

TIME TO SPEAK
The perfect party

LESSON OBJECTIVE
- plan a party

FIND IT

A When do you celebrate? Who do you celebrate with? Do you have parties to celebrate special occasions? What food do people usually eat at celebrations in your country? You can go online to find examples. What's your favorite party food? Why?

B **PREPARE** Imagine you and your partner are party organizers. You are going to organize a party for another pair, your "clients." Ask the other pair these questions to help you decide the type of party you're going to organize.

Your perfect party

Occasion
What are you celebrating?

People
Would you like to invite a lot of people or a few close friends?

Would you like to invite your family?

Place
Do you want to celebrate at home, in a restaurant, or in another place?

Would you like to be inside or outside?

Food
Do you and your friends like to eat spicy food?

Do you prefer to eat fried food or grilled food?

Do you need to think about special diets?

Surprise
Do you like surprises?

C **DECIDE** Use your clients' answers in exercise B to plan your party. Use the phrases at the bottom of the page to help you.

D **DISCUSS** Tell your clients about the party you're planning for them. Then listen to their plans for your party. Say two things you like about the party and two things you would like to change.

E **PRESENT** Present your parties to the class. Which one sounds fun? Which menu is your favorite? Why?

To check your progress, go to page 155.

USEFUL PHRASES

PREPARE
- I'd like that. / I wouldn't like that.
- I'd prefer …
- My brother is a vegetarian/vegan.
- My friend is allergic to nuts/fish/milk, etc.

DECIDE
- Let's invite …
- The party will take place in …
- We'll have … on the menu.

DISCUSS
- I really like that idea.
- I'd love to come to your party!
- It sounds like fun!
- We think you're going to love this.
- What do you think of … ?

UNIT OBJECTIVES

- discuss what to do in your town
- talk about a trip you went on
- give advice and make suggestions
- write advice on living in another country
- plan a short trip

TRIPS

8

START SPEAKING

A **Look at the picture. What adjectives can you use to describe it? Would you like to go there?**

B **Which things are important to you when you're on vacation? Check (✓) your top <u>three</u> choices.**

- ☐ a beautiful place
- ☐ good food
- ☐ doing nothing
- ☐ doing lots of things
- ☐ meeting new people
- ☐ traveling with friends

C **Where did you go on your last vacation? What did you do? Did you have fun? For ideas, watch Celeste's video.**

REAL STUDENT

Does Celeste's vacation sound fun to you?

8.1 HOME–HERE AND THERE

LESSON OBJECTIVE

- discuss what to do in your town

1 VOCABULARY: Traveling

A 2.10 **Look at the pictures. Listen and say the words in the pictures. Which words are (a) people, (b) places, (c) things you bring on vacation, or (d) types of transportation?**

> **!** *luggage* = carry-on bags, suitcases, and large backpacks.

B **Now do the vocabulary exercises for 8.1 on page 148.**

C PAIR WORK **Answer the questions with a partner.**

1 How much do you take with you for a weekend away, one suitcase, a backpack? What about for a long vacation?

2 Do many tourists come to your town? Where do you usually see them?

3 When you visit a new city, do you prefer to use a tourist map or your phone? Do you usually buy a guidebook? Why or why not?

2 LANGUAGE IN CONTEXT

A **Deborah rented a room in her Vancouver home to Nico for five days. Read their reviews of the experience. Did Deborah and Nico enjoy the activities they did together? Why or why not?**

Home Here and There

Review your guest

Nico was a great guest. Most days he explored the city on his own. I gave him a **map** and some **guidebooks**. On the weekend, I was his **tour guide**. I'm always happy to help if my guests want a local guide. We visited lots of interesting landmarks together. When I'm with my guests, I always have a good time. It's like being a **tourist** in my own town!

Review your stay

If you stay in someone's home, you get a good idea of life there. I rented a room in Deborah's apartment. It's right in the heart of downtown. Perfect! Deborah was a great host. On the weekend, I really wanted to go hiking in the mountains, but she took me to a classical music concert instead. Not really my thing. Most days, I borrowed a guidebook from her and explored on my own, so it was OK. Vancouver is a great city!

B PAIR WORK **Circle the words in the reviews on page 76 that mean the following. Add them to your lists in exercise 1A.**

1 a person who is staying in your home
2 to go around a place you don't know
3 the famous and important places in a town or city
4 a person who welcomes a guest into his or her home

C PAIR WORK **Would you like to be a host and have a guest in your home for money? Would you like to rent a room in someone's home when you travel? Why or why not?**

3 GRAMMAR: *if* and *when*

A **Circle the correct options to complete the rules. Use the sentences in the grammar box to help you.**

1 Use ***if*** / ***when*** and the simple present to say that something happens only after another thing happens first.
2 Use ***if*** / ***when*** and the simple present to say that something happens at almost the same time as another thing happens.

if* and *when

I'm always happy to help **if** my guests want a local guide.
When I'm with my guests, I always have a good time.
If you stay in someone's home, you get a good idea of life there.

B **Now go to page 136. Look at the grammar chart and do the grammar exercise for 8.1.**

C PAIR WORK **Complete the sentences so that they are true for you. Then discuss your ideas with a partner. Do you like to do the same things?**

1 When I'm on vacation, I love to … .
2 If the weather is nice on the weekend, I … .
3 When I travel long distances, I like to … .
4 I don't usually … when the weather is cold.

4 SPEAKING

FIND IT

A **Imagine you're a host to some tourists. Think of places to take them in your town. You can go online for ideas. Where is the best place to take them …**

- if they want to eat traditional food? ____________
- if they want to see the sights? ____________
- when it's cold or rainy? ____________
- when it's very hot? ____________
- if they're interested in funny or unusual sights? ____________

B GROUP WORK **Share your ideas with some of your classmates. Do you all agree?**

8.2 TICKET TO RIDE

LESSON OBJECTIVE
- talk about a trip you went on

1 LANGUAGE IN CONTEXT

A 2.11 **Journalist Rosalind Ash took a four-day bus trip from Brazil to Peru. Listen to her video. Which things from the list below does she talk about?**

1 the food ☐ **2** reasons for taking the trip ☐ **3** other passengers ☐

2.11 Audio script

DAY ONE I'm at Tietê bus station in São Paulo, in Brazil, to **catch the bus** for the long trip to Lima, Peru – *5,000* kilometers in *96* hours! It's going to be pretty amazing.

DAY TWO We stopped for lunch at a roadside restaurant and **picked up more passengers**. I met Lucas, who's going to see his girlfriend. He'll **change buses** in Cáceres and go another 200 kilometers north. So many people, so many stories.

DAY THREE It's 1:00 a.m., and we're high up in the mountains now. I think I'm the only person not asleep. Today I talked to a family with three young kids. They **take the bus** once a year to visit their grandparents. They bring a whole suitcase full of books and toys to keep the children happy. Smart parents!

DAY FOUR Just 96 hours later, and we're in Lima! It's great to be here, and to **get off the bus**, but I feel a little sad that it's all over. It was a wonderful experience.

2 VOCABULARY: Using transportation

A **Look at the words in bold in the video text above. Which picture, A, B, or C, do they describe? Write the words in the correct spaces. Can you find Rosalind? And Lucas? And the family she talks to?**

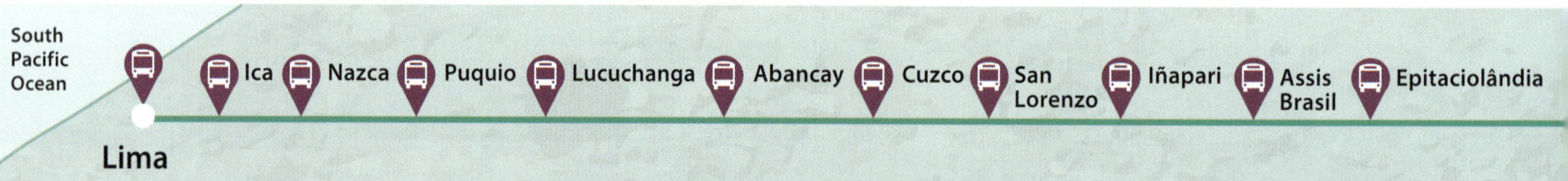

B 2.12 **Read the sentences and write the bold words in the other pictures on page 78. Listen and check your work.**

I **drop** the children **off** at school before I go to work.

When you **get into a taxi**, tell the driver where you want to go.

You can **get on the train** when the doors open.

If you **miss the train**, there's another one soon.

Check the traffic before you **get out of the car**.

C **Now do the vocabulary exercises for 8.2 on page 148.**

FIND IT

D **Would you like to take a four-day trip? Would you prefer to take a car, a bus, or a train? Where would you like to go? Why? You can go online for ideas.**

3 GRAMMAR: Giving reasons using *to* and *for*

A **Circle the correct options to complete the rules. Use the sentences in the grammar box to help you. Underline the reasons in each sentence.**

To give reasons, you can use:

1 *to* + **verb** / **noun** 2 *for* + **verb** / **noun**

Giving reasons using *to* and *for*

They take this trip once a year **to** visit their grandparents.

They bring books and toys **to** keep the children happy.

We stopped **for** lunch.

ACCURACY CHECK

Don't use *for* before *to* + verb.

We went there ~~for~~ to pick up my sister! ✗

We went there to pick up my sister! ✓

B **Now go to page 137. Look at the grammar chart and do the grammar exercise for 8.2.**

C PAIR WORK **Look at the questions. Write as many answers as you can using *to* + verb or *for* + noun. Check your accuracy. Tell another pair of students your answers.**

Why do you use public transportation? (*to go to school*, …)

Why do you go downtown? (*to go shopping*, …)

Why are you studying English? (*for my job*, …)

4 SPEAKING

A **Describe a long trip you took some time in the past. Use the questions to help you prepare.**

- Where did you go?
- Why did you go there?
- How far was it?
- How long did it take?
- What form(s) of transportation did you take? Why?
- How did you feel when you arrived? Why?

B PAIR WORK **Work in pairs. Tell your partner about your journey. For ideas, watch Irene's video.**

I traveled from Bogotá to Caracas. I went to visit a friend and then we went to the coast together for a short vacation. I took the bus. It was a long bus ride!

REAL STUDENT

Does Irene's trip sound fun to you?

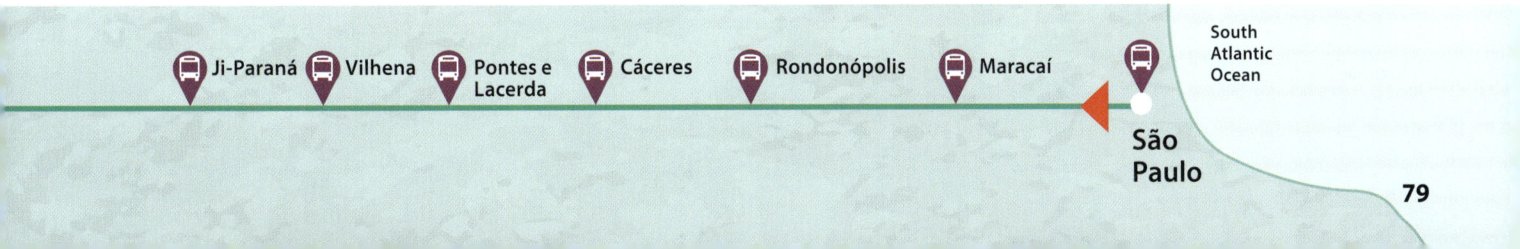

8.3 THAT'S A GREAT IDEA!

LESSON OBJECTIVE
- give advice and make suggestions

1 FUNCTIONAL LANGUAGE

A 2.13 **Read and listen to two conversations. What do the tourists want to know?**

2.13 Audio script

1
A Hi. Tonight is our last night in your beautiful city. Any idea what we can do?
B Your last night? Well, **how about going** to the theater?
A We went to the theater last night.
B **Why don't you go** to the mall? There are some great cafés with live music.
A The mall! **That's a great idea.** How do we get there?
B It's not far – about ten blocks. I can take you there if you'd like.
A Thank you!

2
A Can you tell us how to get to the airport?
B What time is your flight?
A It's at 7:00 p.m. **Should** we **take** a taxi?
B **You could** use the hotel shuttle service. It leaves from here every 30 minutes.
A **That would be great**. How long does it take to get to the airport?
B It takes about 45 minutes. **You should take** the 3:00 p.m. shuttle to get there for 4:00 p.m.
A 3:00 p.m.? **Perfect**! We'll be here. Thanks!

B **Complete the chart with expressions in bold from the conversations above.**

INSIDER ENGLISH

Use *take* for time and for transportation.

*If you **take the bus**, it **takes 30 minutes**.* *When you **take the subway**, it **takes 15**.*

Giving advice and making suggestions	Responding to advice and suggestions
1 ________ to (the theater)?	That's a great 6 ________ !
2 ________ to (the mall)?	That 7 ________ be great.
3 ________ we take a taxi?	3:00 p.m.? 8 ________ !
4 ________ ________ use the hotel shuttle service.	
You 5 ________ take (the 3:00 p.m. shuttle).	

C PAIR WORK **Practice the conversations in exercise 1A with your partner.**

2 REAL-WORLD STRATEGY

A 2.14 **Listen to the hotel receptionist talk to another guest. What two things does she suggest? Which one does the hotel guest decide to do?**

ECHO QUESTIONS

Use echo questions to ask someone to repeat specific information. In an echo question, you repeat the part of the sentence that you hear and then use a question word to ask for the information that you don't hear.

The hotel shuttle to the airport leaves every 30 minutes.
*Sorry, the hotel shuttle leaves **how often**?*

There's a concert in the park tonight.
*Wait, there's a concert **where**?*

B 2.14 **Read the information about echo questions, above. Then look at the sentences from the conversation and complete the questions. Listen again and check.**

A How about going to the mall?
B Going [1] ________________ ?

A You could go to the museum. It opens at 10:00, so you don't have long to wait.
B Wait, it opens [2] ________________________ ?

C PAIR WORK **Student A: Go to page 158. Student B: Go to page 160. Follow the instructions.**

3 PRONUNCIATION: Saying long and short vowel sounds

A 2.15 **Listen. Which word sounds shorter? Which is the last sound in this word?**

1 great 2 grade

B 2.16 **Listen and check (✓) the words that sound longer.**

1 ☐ tried ☐ flight
2 ☐ night ☐ side
3 ☐ art ☐ award
4 ☐ need ☐ meet

C PAIR WORK **Practice the sentences with a partner.**

1 I need to eat.
2 Why don't we meet?
3 We could meet in the street.
4 How about meeting in the street for something to eat?

4 SPEAKING

A **Imagine some tourists stop you on the street outside your home. They ask you for advice. Choose one of the situations below and think of two or three suggestions for the tourists.**

1 They want to get to the main square downtown. They don't want to take a taxi.
2 They need to go to the train station as quickly as possible.
3 They're hungry and looking for a place to eat quickly and cheaply.
4 They want to see the best parts, but they don't want to walk.

B PAIR WORK **Student A: You are the tourist. Ask for help. Student B: Offer your advice. Student A: Respond to the suggestions. Then reverse the roles and use a different situation.**

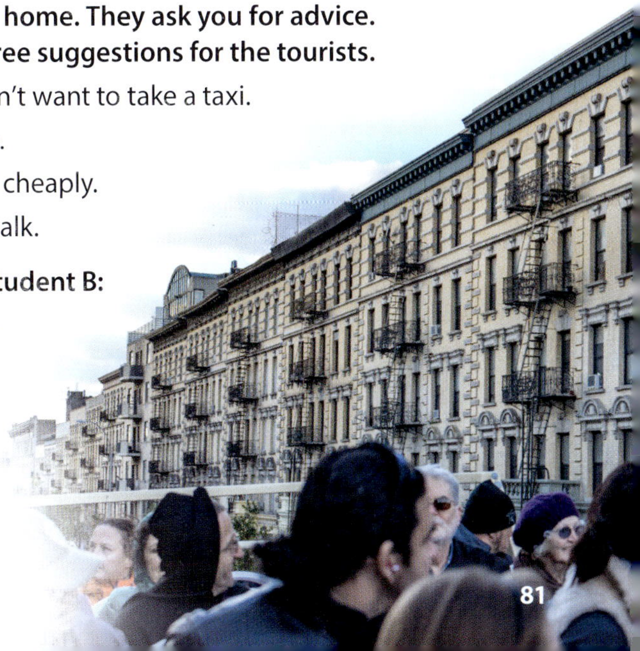

8.4 LEAVING HOME

LESSON OBJECTIVE

- write advice on living in another country

1 LISTENING

A PAIR WORK **Imagine that a friend is leaving in six months to live in another country. What three pieces of advice can you give him/her? Discuss with your partner.**

B 2.17 LISTEN FOR GIST **Listen to four people giving advice to people who are going to live in another country. Is their advice the same as yours?**

C 2.17 LISTEN FOR DETAIL **Listen again. What advice does each caller give? Write 1, 2, 3, or 4.**

1 Learn the language. [1]
2 Get to know your way around with maps. [ ]
3 Find a good place to live. [ ]
4 Work with a conversation partner. [ ]
5 Ask friends or family about local customs. [ ]
6 Get to know people. [ ]
7 Join clubs or groups that fit your interests. [ ]

D PAIR WORK THINK CRITICALLY **People don't always choose to move to another country. Think of reasons why people leave their home countries. What extra problems do they usually face?**

2 PRONUNCIATION: Listening for intonation

A 2.18 **Listen. Focus on the rising intonation and falling intonation of the speaker's voice.**

If you have any family friends or contacts in the country, ask them to help.

B 2.19 **Draw arrows to show the rising intonation ↗ and the falling intonation ↘. Listen and check.**

1 When you join a language club, you can learn very quickly.

2 If you can, try and find a place before you go.

3 If you like hiking, join a hiking club.

C **Circle the correct option to complete the sentence.**

Speakers' voices often go up to show they're *finished / not finished*.

3 WRITING

A Read the listeners' comments. What extra advice do they offer? Do you agree with the advice? Which do you think is the best advice?

Advice Forum

Profile | Messages | FAQS | Sign out

New posts

On today's "Backpack Nation," four listeners offered some advice for when you go to live in another country. What did you think of their ideas? Do you have any advice to give?

Reply

Thank you for the advice. It's a great idea to join a language club. **You could also offer** to give lessons in your own language. It's a good way to meet people and to make some extra money at the same time!

I agree that a comfortable place to live is really important. **I think it's a good idea** to get a room in an apartment or house with other people. You make friends, you practice the language, and it costs less. It worked for me!

Great advice, thanks! **I think it's also very important** to remember to stay in touch with your friends and family back home when you first arrive. If you don't, you can get really lonely. The internet makes it so easy. When I lived away from home, I talked to my family every day. It really helped!

B Read the comments again. Check (✓) the things the people do in their comments.

1 Thank the speakers for their advice. ☐
2 Refer to a piece of advice from the speakers. ☐
3 Agree with the speakers' advice. ☐
4 Disagree with the speakers' advice. ☐
5 Speak from experience. ☐

C PAIR WORK Look at the phrases in **bold** in the comments. Write three pieces of advice using the three phrases. You can use your ideas from exercise 1A to help you.

WRITE IT

D WRITING SKILL Write a short comment on one of the pieces of advice in the listening (page 82) or in the reading text (above). Include at least three points from the checklist.

☐ Refer to the advice giver.
☐ Agree or disagree with a piece of advice.
☐ Offer your own advice.
☐ Explain how your advice will help.
☐ Give an example from your own experience or from someone you know.

E Read your classmates' comments. Did anyone give the same advice as you? Whose advice did you like the most?

8.5

TIME TO SPEAK

Planning a trip

LESSON OBJECTIVE

- plan a short trip

A **RESEARCH** Look at the pictures of popular tourist destinations. What types of places or events are they? Think of three more big events that people travel to. Why do people go to these places? Which place would you like to go to? Why?

B Choose a destination that you would all like to go to. Think of some different things to see. What activities would you like to do?

C **PREPARE** You are going on a trip for three days. Decide what you want to do on each day. Make sure you include activities for all the different tastes and interests of your group. Plan how you'll travel between activities. Make a table like the one below and take notes.

Destination: ______

	Travel	Activities	Things to see
Day 1			
Day 2			
Day 3			

D **PRESENT** Tell the class about your plans. Listen to the other groups. Which vacations sound the most relaxing? The most active? The most fun? Which would you most like to go on? Why?

To check your progress, go to page 155.

USEFUL PHRASES

RESEARCH
It looks like a …
What can we do there?

PREPARE
Let's go to …
What do you want to do there?
I suggest …
Why don't we eat/watch/play …

PRESENT
First, we …
After that … / Then … / Next …
Finally …

UNIT OBJECTIVES

- compare stores and what they sell
- talk about people in photos
- ask for and give opinions
- write a paragraph describing a photo
- create and present an ad

LOOKING GOOD

9

START SPEAKING

A Look at the picture. What's he doing? Do you do this?

B Think about yourself and your friends. Do you think a lot about the clothes you wear and how you look? How many times a day do you look at yourself (in mirrors, pictures, selfies, store windows, etc.)? For ideas, watch Alessandra's video.

C *A picture is worth a thousand words*. What does this mean? Do you agree? Are pictures important to you? Why?

REAL STUDENT

Are you the same as Alessandra?

9.1 WHAT TO WEAR AT WORK

LESSON OBJECTIVE
- compare stores and what they sell

1 VOCABULARY: Naming accessories

A 2.20 PAIR WORK **Listen and say the words. Which items do you have? Tell a partner.**

B **Now do the vocabulary exercises for 9.1 on page 149.**

C **Put the accessories in order from head to feet. Do you and your partner agree on the order?**

2 LANGUAGE IN CONTEXT

A **Look at the pictures. What are they wearing? Now read an email from Mike to a friend. In the pictures, which one is Mike, and which one is his new coworker?**

Hi Angelica,

Well, here I am in Berlin! I still can't believe it – I had an interview one month ago, and I started work today!

So far, Europe's OK, very pretty. But the weather is worse than at home – colder, wetter, windier – horrible! For my first day on the job, I wore my winter suit with a blue **tie**.

I didn't know it, but the dress code at this company is a lot less formal than at my old company. **Sneakers** and T-shirts for almost everyone. A lot of the men wear **bracelets** and **earrings**! And everything is more modern than at my old office. The work is more or less the same, but the people are much warmer and friendlier than in my old office. Maybe it's the sneakers!

It's definitely a more interesting place to work, and the money is better, too. I'm really lucky. But I'm going to need to buy some casual clothes!

Mike

GLOSSARY
formal (*adj*) traditional, serious
casual (*adj*) relaxed, not formal

B **Read the email again. Check (✓) the sentence(s) that are true. Correct the false ones.**

- ☐ 1 The new office is different from his old office.
- ☐ 2 The people in his new job aren't very friendly.
- ☐ 3 Some things in his new office aren't so good.
- ☐ 4 He prefers the weather in Berlin.

C GROUP WORK **What do business people usually wear to work where you live? Would you prefer to work in an office where appearance is important? Why? For ideas, watch Caio's video.**

REAL STUDENT

Do you agree with Caio?

3 GRAMMAR: Comparative adjectives

A **Answer the questions. Use the sentences in the grammar box to help you.**

1 Which word do you use after a comparative adjective to compare two or more things?

____

2 What are the opposites of ***more formal*** and ***less modern***?

______________________ ______________________

3 What are the comparatives of ***good*** and ***bad***?

______________________ ______________________

Comparative adjectives

Everything is **more modern than** at my old office.
The weather is **worse than** at home.
It's **colder**, **wetter**, **windier**.

The dress code is a lot **less formal**.
The money is **better**.

! *more* = > *less* = <

B **Now go to page 137. Look at the grammar chart and do the grammar exercise for 9.1.**

C **Put the adjectives in parentheses in the comparative form to make sentences that are true for you. Use *than* and *less* when necessary. Then check your accuracy.**

1 People usually look ______________________ in black clothes. (formal)
2 In winter, warm gloves are ______________________ a hat. (important)
3 A necklace is ______________________ a scarf. (expensive)
4 Colored sneakers are ______________________ white ones. (cool)
5 People look ______________________ when they wear ties. (serious)

✓ ACCURACY CHECK

Don't use *more* and *-er* together.

Your sunglasses are ~~more better~~ than mine. ✗
Your sunglasses are better than mine. ✓

D PAIR WORK **Do you agree with your partner's sentences in exercise 3C?**

I think black is boring. I wear lots of different colors.

Really? I think black is cool. It looks good on everyone!

4 SPEAKING

FIND IT

GROUP WORK **Think of two places in your town where you can buy clothes and fashion accessories. Go online for ideas if you want. Compare these places and the things they sell. Use the adjectives in the box or your own ideas.**

beautiful	cheap/expensive	fashionable	friendly	good/bad	interesting

9.2 BABY PHOTOS

LESSON OBJECTIVE
- talk about people in photos

1 VOCABULARY: Describing appearance

A 2.21 **Listen and say the words.**

B PAIR WORK **Imagine you're designing your own avatar. Use the features in exercise 1A. Describe your avatar to your partner. How is your avatar's appearance different from your real appearance?**

C **Now do the vocabulary exercises for 9.2 on page 149.**

D PAIR WORK **Think of a famous man and a famous woman. Describe them to your partner. Can they guess who you're describing? Now compare the two people (who has longer hair, darker hair, etc.).**

She is a young woman with very long hair.

Is her hair darker or lighter than the other person?

2 LANGUAGE IN CONTEXT

A PAIR WORK **Think about a picture of you as a child. Describe it to your partner.**

B 2.22 **Listen to the conversation between Pete, Pete's mom, and Pete's new girlfriend, Ava. Describe Pete's appearance as a baby and as a teenager. How does Pete feel about the photos now?**

2.22 Audio script

Mom Ava, would you like to see some pictures of Pete when he was younger?

Pete Mom, please …

Mom Look. This one is when Pete was two. Isn't he the cutest little baby with his **dark, straight hair** and funny smile?

Ava Yes!

Mom This is the funniest one. He was 15, and he had a little **mustache**. He couldn't grow a real **beard**, of course. He was the youngest boy in the class, but you wanted to look older. He was the most sensitive child.

Pete Mom, why do you always want to show people the worst pictures of me?

Mom Now, where is my favorite one, you know, from when you were 12 months old? You in the bath. It's here somewhere …

Pete No, not that one, Mom. Please …

Mom Here it is! It's the best one of all!

Pete Oh, no.

3 GRAMMAR: Superlative adjectives

A **Circle the correct options to complete the rules. Use the sentences in the grammar box to help you.**

1 Superlative adjectives usually begin with ***a / the***.

2 Superlatives compare **two things / three or more things**.

3 Short superlatives end with ***-er / -est***. Longer superlatives begin with ***the most / more***.

4 The superlative of *good* is ***the best / the worst***. The superlative of *bad* is ***the best / the worst***.

Superlative adjectives

Isn't he **the cutest** little baby?
He was **the most sensitive** child.
Why do you always want to show people **the worst** pictures of me?
This is **the best** one of all.

B **Now go to page 137. Look at the grammar chart and do the grammar exercise for 9.2.**

C PAIR WORK **Put the adjectives in parentheses in the superlative form. Then answer the questions and give some details about each person. Tell your partner.**

Which of your friends or family members has …

1 the ______________ eyes? (beautiful)
2 the ______________ beard? (big)
3 the ______________ makeup? (cool)
4 the ______________ hair? (curly)
5 the ______________ hair? (dark)
6 the ______________ smile? (friendly)
7 the ______________ clothes? (good)
8 the ______________ jewelry? (interesting)

My cousin Ramon has the best clothes. He always wears sunglasses and cool shoes.

4 SPEAKING

FIND IT

PAIR WORK **Find <u>three</u> pictures of the same person (you or another person) on your phone. Show the pictures to your partner and give an opinion about each one using superlatives. Does your partner agree?**

Here are three pictures of me. I think this is the best one. I like it because I have a happy smile and my hair looks good. It's a picture of me on vacation at the beach last year. That was the most fantastic vacation of my life. What do you think? Is this the best of the pictures?

9.3 WHAT DO YOU THINK OF THIS?

LESSON OBJECTIVE
- ask for and give opinions

1 FUNCTIONAL LANGUAGE

A 2.23 **Read and listen to the conversations. What are the people making decisions about?**

INSIDER ENGLISH

Use *go with* to say that two things match.

*Does this belt **go with** these pants?*

2.23 Audio script

1 A **What do you think of** this scarf, Sam?
B **It looks nice**, Fiona! Really nice.
A **Don't you think it's** kind of bright?
B It's a little bright, **I guess**, but not too much. And it goes with your dress.
A **How do you feel about** this white one?
B **I prefer** the other one.
A This one?
B Yes. **It's perfect**! And it's cheaper, too.

2 A I'm thinking of using this picture for my blog. **Do you like it**?
B **I'm not sure.** You don't seem very happy.
A I'm smiling in the photo! How about this one?
B **That one is** better, but **isn't it** a little formal?
A Really? Can you look and choose the best one?
B Sure.

B **Complete the chart with expressions in bold from the conversations above.**

Asking for an opinion	Giving a positive opinion	Giving a negative or neutral opinion
What do you [1] ______ this? How do you feel [2] ______? Do you [3] ______ it?	It [4] ______ nice. I [5] ______ the other one. It's [6] ______! [7] ______ is better.	Don't you [8] ______ it's (kind of bright)? I [9] ______. I'm not [10] ______. [11] ______ it (a little formal)?

C PAIR WORK **Practice the conversations in exercise 1A with a partner.**

2 REAL-WORLD STRATEGY

A 2.24 **Listen to another conversation between Sam and Fiona. What item is Fiona trying to choose?**

B 2.24 **Complete Fiona's opinion of Sam's suggestion below. Listen again and check. Is her opinion positive?**

Sam How do you feel about these? **Fiona** They're OK, ______________.

I GUESS

Use *I guess* when you're not certain about something or if you don't have a strong opinion.

Don't you think these shoes go perfectly with this dress?

I guess, but I like your brown sandals with it, too.

C 2.25 PAIR WORK **Read the information about *I guess* in the box above. Then write it in the correct places in the conversations below. Listen and check. Then practice the sentences with a partner.**

1 A I think these earrings are great ______________.
  B They're OK, I guess.
2 A This belt is OK, ______________. But it's nothing special.
  B ______________ I think it's perfect.
3 A You look really serious in that picture ______________. I prefer this one.
  B Yeah, ______________ it's better than the other one.

3 PRONUNCIATION: Saying /ɜ/ vowel sound

A 2.26 **Listen. Underline the parts of the words with the /ɜ/ vowel sound.**

1 prefer 2 shirt 3 perfect

B PAIR WORK **Say one of the words in each group. Your partner listens and circle the word you say. Then switch roles.**

1 a bird b bed 2 a turn b ten 3 a heard b head

C 2.27 **Underline the words with the /ɜ/ sound. Listen and check, and practice the conversation with a partner.**

A What do you think of this red shirt?
B Turn around … Hmm, I'm not sure.
A How do you feel about this green shirt?
B I prefer the first shirt.

4 SPEAKING

GROUP WORK **Look at the pictures and discuss your opinions. Use the functional language to help you.**

What do you think of that shirt?

I think it's awful! I prefer the one on the right. How do you feel about that one?

It's kind of fun, I guess.

9.4 IMAGE IS EVERYTHING

LESSON OBJECTIVE
- write a paragraph describing a photo

1 READING

A **THINK BEFORE YOU READ** Look at the pictures from different car ads. What do the pictures say about the cars? Which images do you like the most?

1 
2 
3 
4 

B **READ FOR MAIN IDEAS** Look at the different types of people and match them to the pictures in exercise 1A. Then read the article and match the people to the paragraphs.

a The happy family
b The driver of the future
c The cool city person
d The freedom lover

How to sell ... CARS

Advertisers don't just sell *things*. They sell *ideas*. Here are the four most important ways that car companies use images to connect with buyers.

1 ______

A car is speeding along a beautiful open road near the ocean, in the desert, or in the mountains. The air is clean and, most important of all, there are no other cars.

Picture ☐

2 ______

Dad is driving, mom is smiling, and the two kids in the back seat are laughing. The car is full of things for a weekend trip to the beach – toys, towels, snacks – but there's always room for more.

Picture ☐

3 ______

The driver is wearing fashionable clothes, and her best friend is sitting beside her. They're listening to music as she drives. The car is small, easy to drive, easier to park and fun.

Picture ☐

4 ______

Is this a car or a spaceship? This car is full of the most modern technology possible – cameras, screens, an entertainment system, GPS. The car almost drives by itself, and it doesn't need gas, just electricity!

Picture ☐

C **PAIR WORK** **THINK CRITICALLY** Discuss the ways that the car ads in the article are different from reality. Look at the ideas in the box and add two more.

Some families are not happy on long car trips.
It's often difficult to find any parking space, big or small.

2 WRITING

A Read the information about a contest. Then read the email below. Which kind of customer is this image for? Do you like this person's idea? Why or why not?

Reply Forward

The car is in a street where people live. It's a small car, perfect for the city. Someone is cleaning the car. He or she is very proud of it. The idea is that the car is very important to the person because it's very practical, but it also looks good.

B Read another submission to the contest. Divide the text into four sentences with correct punctuation. Check your work by looking at exercise 2A. What kind of customer are these images for?

> my image is of a beach on a warm summer day the car is parked and the driver is getting beach things out of the back the driver's door is open and her dog is already running to the beach this image gives the idea of being young and full of energy

C WRITING SKILLS Look at these other submissions. The sentences are too long, and the writers did not use any periods. Change the texts into two or three sentences. Don't forget the capital letters.

1 the most important thing in my image is the famous football player next to the car he is standing with a football in one hand and the key to the car in the other

2 my image shows an open door of the car you can see the inside of the car it looks very modern and nice

WRITE IT

D Prepare your ideas for the contest. Describe your image. Use these phrases to help you.

My image shows …
The most important thing in my image is …
The car is driving on a …
There are no other cars in the image …

E GROUP WORK Share your submission and image with the rest of the class. Which images and ideas do you like most?

9.5

TIME TO SPEAK
Sell it!

LESSON OBJECTIVE
- create and present an ad

A RESEARCH **Look at the pictures. What do you see? What do you think they are selling?**

B DISCUSS **Here are some of the most popular people and things in advertisements. Why do you think they are popular? Use the phrases at the bottom of the page to help you.**

- animals
- babies and children
- perfect families
- friends having fun
- beautiful people
- funny or romantic stories

C DECIDE **Look at the list of products and agree on the two most interesting ones.**

an airline	candy	jeans
perfume	a smartphone	soda

D PREPARE **Choose one of your products and make an ad for it. The ad can be print (magazine, poster) or a video (for TV or online). Think about these questions as you plan it.**

- Who is the ad for? (parents, teenagers, etc.)
- Who is in the ad? What are they wearing?
- Where is the ad? (in the mountains, in a house, etc.)
- What happens in the ad?
- What do the people say?
- What kind of music is in the ad?
- Are there words in the ad? What do they say?

E PRESENT **Present your ad to the class. When all the presentations are finished, have an awards ceremony. Vote on the best ads in these categories:**

- the funniest ad
- the most interesting ad
- the most creative ad
- the best ad

To check your progress, go to page 155.

USEFUL PHRASES

DISCUSS

In my opinion … / I'd say that …

I love ads with … because …

I think those ads are funny/cute/annoying/stupid.

DECIDE

Let's do/choose/think about …

I think we should …

PRESENT

Our ad starts with …

People are going to remember our ad because …

REVIEW 3 (UNITS 7–9)

1 VOCABULARY

A **Complete the chart with words from the box.**

burger   bus station   gloves   onion   roasted   scarf   spicy   suitcase

cereal	bitter	airplane	belt
chicken	boiled	backpack	bracelet
jam	delicious	check-in	earrings
lettuce	grilled	guidebook	necklace
strawberry	sour	map	tie
1 ______	3 ______	5 ______	7 ______
2 ______	4 ______	6 ______	8 ______

B **Write a category for each group of words above. Then add at least two more words or phrases to each group.**

2 GRAMMAR

A **Complete the conversation.**

A Excuse me, can you help me? I can't find my little sister, Nell. I went to the café [1]*for / to* a burger and [2]*a / some* fries for us. Nell wanted [3]*for / to* stay outside. She always waits for me [4]*where / when* I go somewhere. Normally, she doesn't mind [5]*be / being* alone for a [6]*some / few* minutes. But now I can't find her.

B It's all right. I'll help you. Describe her to me.

A Well, she's ten years old. She has dark hair – it's longer [7]*for / than* mine, and it's [8]*curlier / curliest*. She's wearing jeans and a pink T-shirt. It's [9]*more / the most* colorful T-shirt you can imagine! Oh, and she doesn't speak [10]*some / any* English.

B Don't worry. A lot [11]*the / of* children get lost, and we always find them. The [12]*better / best* thing to do is wait here. I'm going to contact the security officers, OK?

B PAIR WORK **Practice reading the conversation with a partner. Change the details and make a new conversation.**

3 SPEAKING

A PAIR WORK **Think of a special place that you enjoy going to -- a park, a shopping mall, an amusement park, etc. Work with a partner and discuss the questions. Make notes on your partner's answers.**

- Why do you enjoy going there? What do you like to do there?
- Can you think of three different reasons that people go to this place?
- When you go to this place, what are the first things you do?
- Is it very close to your home? What is the easiest way to get there?
- Is it better to go on the weekend or during the week? Why? What is the best time of day to go?

I like to go to a little park near the river. It's a good place for…

4 FUNCTIONAL LANGUAGE

A **Read the conversation in a hotel. Complete the conversation with the phrases from the box.**

could you recommend	how about	how was it	I'd like	if you want, you can
I guess	we prefer	what do you think	what kind of	you could

A Excuse me, [1] ______________ a place for dinner?

B Sure. [2] ______________ food do you like?

A It doesn't matter to my husband, but I think [3] ______________ something Italian.

B Well, [4] ______________ try the pizzeria across the street, or [5] ______________ eat at the hotel restaurant. We have pasta dishes.

A [6] ______________ of the pizzeria? Is it good?

B It's okay, [7] ______________, but I think the hotel restaurant is better.

A [8] ______________ somewhere different. We ate here yesterday.

B Well, there's Bella Napoli, that new Italian place near the park. I went there last week. [9] ______________ that?

A [10] ______________?

B It was really nice.

B PAIR WORK **Practice reading the conversation in pairs. Then change the details to make a new conversation.**

5 SPEAKING

A PAIR WORK **Choose one of the situations. Act it out in pairs.**

1 You are preparing a dish that you really like. Tell your friend about the dish. Then ask for an opinion and advice. Your friend suggests ways of improving it.

A Here, taste this. What do you think?

B Mm, delicious! And very spicy.

2 You brought your friend to your family's celebration. All your favorite foods are there. Tell your friend about the foods and say which are the best, and why. Answer your friend's questions, too.

A My grandmother makes the most delicious desserts.

B I love sweet things! What's in this one? …

B **Change roles and repeat the role play.**

UNIT OBJECTIVES

- talk about how to avoid danger at work
- make predictions about your future
- describe a medical problem and ask for help
- write an email to your future self
- plan a reality TV show

RISKY BUSINESS

10

START SPEAKING

A **What can you see in the picture? Would you like to do this? Why or why not?**

B **Which of these dangerous or scary things do you enjoy? Think of three more things.**

amusement parks | dark places | extreme sports | fast cars | horror movies

C **What things are you afraid of? For ideas, watch Celeste's video.**

REAL STUDENT

Are you afraid of the same things as Celeste?

10.1 DANGER ON THE JOB

LESSON OBJECTIVE
- talk about how to avoid danger at work

1 VOCABULARY: Describing jobs

A 2.28 PAIR WORK **Listen and repeat the jobs. Which ones are the most dangerous?**

accountant	architect	call center worker	dentist	engineer
IT specialist	lawyer	mechanic	nurse	paramedic
photographer	physical therapist	police officer	project manager	receptionist

B 2.29 **Which jobs from the list in exercise 1A are in the pictures? Label them. Then listen and check.**

A

______

B
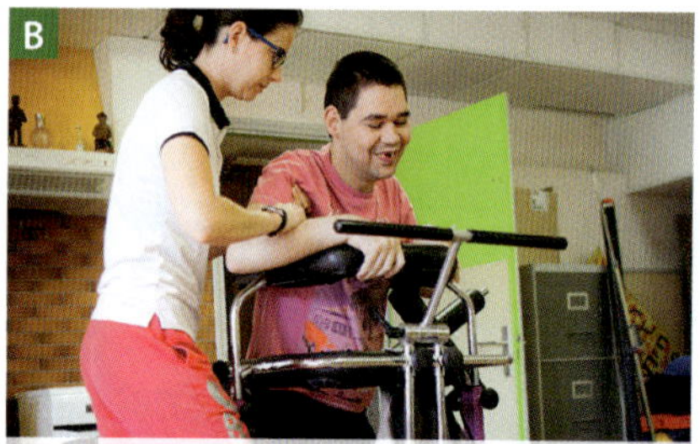
______

C

______

D

______

E
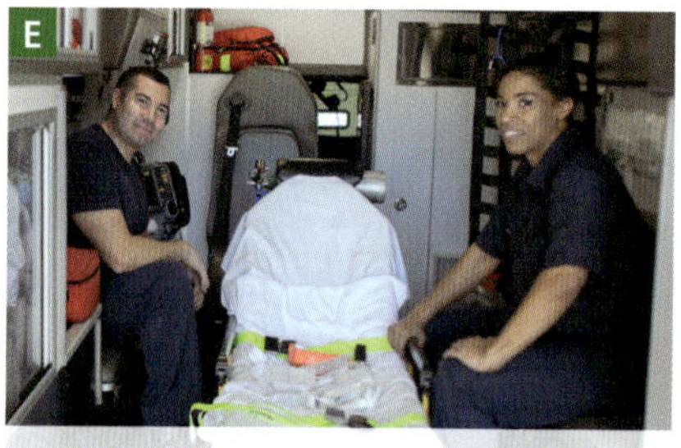
______

F

______

C **Now do the vocabulary exercises for 10.1 on page 150.**

2 LANGUAGE IN CONTEXT

A **Look at the title of the article. Which jobs in exercise 1A is it talking about? Read and check your answers.**

B GROUP WORK **Think of (a) a person you know who has one of the jobs in exercise 1A and (b) a person who has a dangerous job. Is it the same person? Do they like their job(s)? Why or why not?**

GLOSSARY
microbe *(n)* a tiny life form, including bacteria, viruses, and fungi.
square inch *(n)* a unit of measurement. 1 in^2 = 6.5 cm^2.

DANGER AT WORK!

I'm an office worker. I spend my working life at my computer. It's not physically difficult, but it's not without danger. Dr. Charles Gerba, a germ expert from the University of Arizona, says there are millions of invisible enemies all around us ...

A Viruses love offices. Air-conditioning systems recycle air and the germs in it. When one person in the office has a cold, their germs are on 40–60% of their coworkers in just four hours. The virus can stay in the office for three days!

B Some keyboards are dirtier than toilet seats – fact! Dr. Gerba did a study of more than 100 offices (law offices, call centers, accountant services, etc.) and found keyboards with 3,295 microbes per square inch. For toilet seats, that number is usually about 49 microbes!

Why? Food falls into your keyboard and produces bacteria. Dr. Gerba calls the keyboard a "bacteria cafeteria." Next lunchtime, ask yourself: "Do I really have to eat at my desk?"

3 GRAMMAR: *have to*

A Circle the options to complete the sentences. Use the sentences in the grammar box to help you. Match each point to a paragraph in the article on page 98.

1 It **is** / **isn't** necessary to clean your keyboard. ___

2 It **is** / **isn't** necessary to stay home when you have a cold. ___

have to

a You **have to** clean your keyboard.

b You **don't have to** stay home when you have a cold, but it's better if you do.

B Now go to page 138. Look at the grammar chart and do the grammar exercise for 10.1.

ACCURACY CHECK

The negative form is *don't / doesn't have to*.
Use *do / does* in short answers.

I don't have to go to school today.
Really? I ~~have~~. ✗
I don't have to go to school today.
Really? I do. ✓

C Complete the questions with the correct form of *have to*. Then check your accuracy. Ask your partner the questions and take notes. Then tell a new partner about your first partner's answers.

1 you / work / long hours? How many hours / you / work?
Do you have to work long hours? How many hours do you have to work?

2 What time / you / start / work?
___

3 you / wear / special clothes? Why?
___

4 What kind of dangers / you / face / in your work?
___

5 you / get / any special training? What kind?
___

4 SPEAKING

FIND IT

GROUP WORK Think of a dangerous job that was not in this lesson. What dangers do people with this job have? What can they do to make their job safer? You can use your phone to find pictures and information.

Zookeepers have to work with dangerous animals. They have to clean up after the animals. To be safer, they have to put the animals in another place when they clean.

10.2 DON'T WORRY, DAD

LESSON OBJECTIVE

- make predictions about your future

1 VOCABULARY: Describing health problems

A 2.30 **Listen and say the phrases. Find the problems in the pictures, circle them, and draw a line to the correct phrase.**

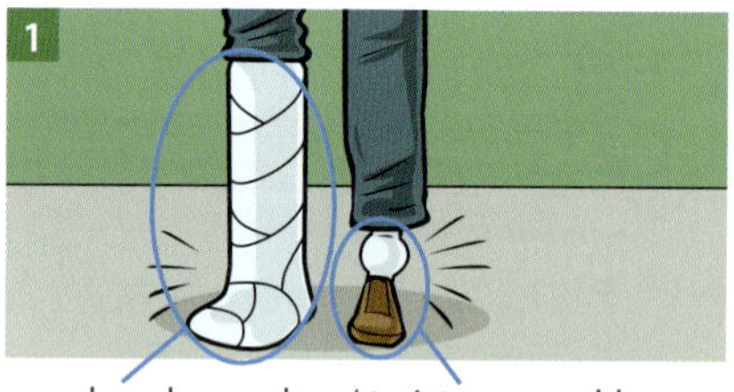

break your leg / twist your ankle

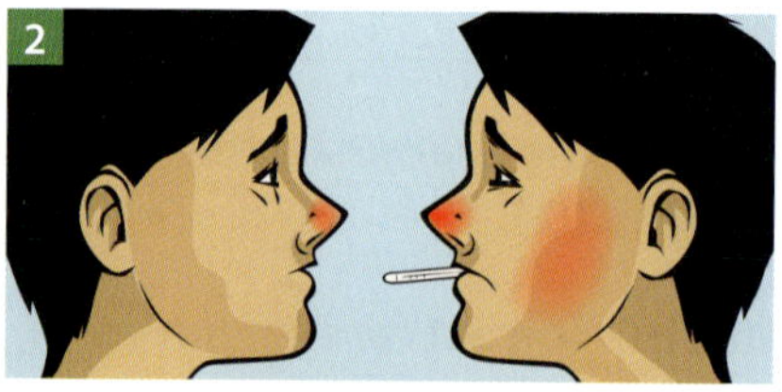

catch a cold / the flu

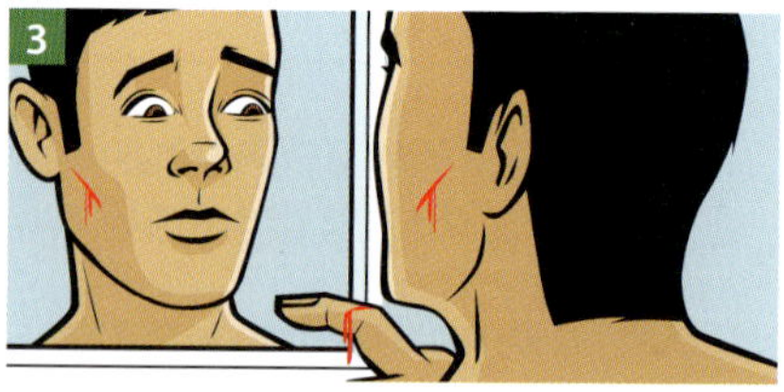

cut your finger / yourself shaving

have a headache / toothache / stomachache

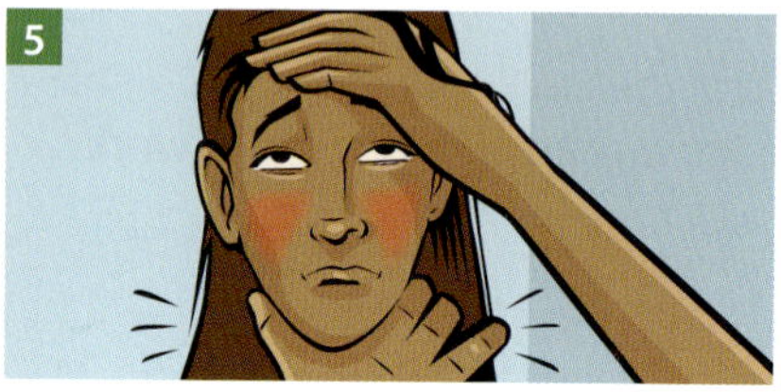

have a fever / sore throat

hurt your back / bang your head

B PAIR WORK **Put the health problems in exercise 1A into two groups: INJURY (something that happens because of an accident) and ILLNESS (a way to be sick).**

C **Now do the vocabulary exercises for 10.2 on page 150.**

2 LANGUAGE IN CONTEXT

A 2.31 **Amelia's father is worried about her. Listen and say why.**

2.31 Audio script

Father Are you ready, Amelia? Do you have everything? Will you be OK?

Amelia Dad, I'm going to work, not the moon. I'll be fine.

Father But it's your first day in a new job. Do you have your headache pills? You might have a headache later. Or hurt your back. I mean, all day in front of a computer.

Amelia I won't need anything, Dad.

Father How do you know? A new job, new people, new everything. It's a stressful situation. You might need something for that.

Amelia It's a new experience, that's all.

Father Will they give you anything to eat? You'll have a stomachache if you don't eat. And you'll probably be tired later in the day. Here's an energy drink.

Amelia Thanks, Dad.

Father Be careful!

Amelia Love you, Dad!

B 2.31 **Listen again and read. Which health problems from exercise 1A does Amelia's father worry about?**

C PAIR WORK **Think of someone (a friend or a member of your family) who worries a lot. Give examples of things they say.**

3 GRAMMAR: Making predictions

A **Complete the rules. Use the sentences in the grammar box to help you.**

1 We use ***will*** / ________________ to make predictions about the future.

2 When we are not sure, we use ________________ or ________________ .

Making predictions

Will you be OK?	You **might** have a headache later.
I'**ll** be fine.	You **may** need something for that.
I **won't** need anything.	

B **Now go to page 138. Look at the grammar chart and do the grammar exercise for 10.2.**

C PAIR WORK **Read the situations and make <u>three</u> predictions for each one using the words in the box.**

may maybe might possibly probably will/'ll won't

1 It's Silvia's first day in her new job in a call center. She has a headache, and feels stressed.

____

2 Benny has a stomachache and a fever. He has an important job interview later in the day.

____

3 Vera is running to work because she's late. It's very cold and there's snow on the ground.

____

4 SPEAKING

A **You're going to ask a partner to make predictions about his/her future. Prepare your questions. Use the topics in the box or your own ideas.**

family life health home studies work

Five years from now, do you think you'll live in a house or an apartment?

When will you retire from work?

B PAIR WORK **Ask your questions from exercise 4A. Listen to your partner's answers. Say something positive about your partner's predictions. For ideas, watch Caio's video.**

REAL STUDENT

Which predictions are more positive: Caio's or your partner's?

I think I'll live in an apartment. I won't have enough money to buy a house.

Well, maybe your apartment will be big and really nice.

10.3 WHAT'S THE MATTER?

LESSON OBJECTIVE
- describe a medical problem and ask for help

1 FUNCTIONAL LANGUAGE

A 2.32 **Read and listen to the conversations. What does the person need in each conversation?**

2.32 Audio script

1 A **What's wrong**?
B I really don't feel well, Anna. It feels like my throat is blocked.
A **What's the matter**? Are you allergic to something?
B No. It's my asthma. I can't breathe. **My chest hurts**.
A **What do you want me to do**?
B I need my inhaler. **Can you** get it for me?
A Where is it?
B It's on my desk.
A Yes, sure. I'll be right back.

2 A Good morning, ma'am. **How can I help** you?
B **I need** something for my head.
A **Where exactly does it hurt**?
B **It hurts here** at the front. It's like something is squeezing my head. And **I have a pain** behind my eyes, too.
A **What happened**? Did you bang your head or have an accident?
B No, nothing like that. It's just a headache, but the pain is killing me.
A OK. I can give you some tablets. Take two of these every four hours.

INSIDER ENGLISH
The pain is killing me = It hurts a lot.

B **Complete the chart with expressions in bold from the conversations above.**

Offering help	Asking for information about the problem	Asking someone for help
[1] ________ ________ I help you? [2] ________ ________ ________ want me to do?	What's [3] ________? What's the [4] ________? Where exactly [5] ________ ________ ________? What [6] ________?	[7] ________ ________ get it for me? [8] ________ ________ something (for my head).

Describing symptoms		
My (chest) [9] ________.	It [10] ________ here.	I have a [11] ________ behind my eyes.

C PAIR WORK **Practice the conversations in exercise 1A with your partner.**

2 REAL-WORLD STRATEGY

A 2.33 **Listen to another conversation in a drugstore. What is the customer's problem? Why does he have this problem?**

B 2.33 **Read the information about how to describe pain, below. Listen to the conversation again and check (✓) the expression the customer uses to describe his pain. Write the complete phrase the customer uses.**

IT'S LIKE / IT FEELS LIKE

When we're not sure about a medical problem or don't know the name of it, we can say *it is like* or *it feels like* something else.

☐ *It's like* ______________________

☐ *It feels* ______________________

____

C **Rearrange the words to make sentences.**

1 a / in / It's / knife / like / my stomach ______________________
2 a / bright / eyes / in / It's / light / like / my ______________________
3 broken / feels / It / like / it's ______________________
4 feels / hit / It / like / me / someone ______________________

3 PRONUNCIATION: Saying final consonant sounds

A 2.34 **Say these sounds together. Then listen and say the words.**

1 /s/ and /t/ = /st/	3 /n/ and /d/ = /nd/	5 /k/ and /t/ = /kt/
2 /s/ and /k/ = /sk/	4 /n/ and /s/ = /ns/	6 /t/ and /s/ = /ts/

B 2.35 **Listen. Focus on the ends of the words. Which word has the same final consonant sound as the example word? (Circle) it.**

1 *chest*:	(stressed)	exercised
2 *desk*:	twist	risk
3 *happened*:	accountant	weekend
4 *ambulance*:	experience	accident
5 *blocked*:	architect	dentist
6 *hurts*:	sports	cleaned

C PAIR WORK **Work with a partner. Practice the conversations. Focus on the final consonant sounds.**

1 **A** What happe**ned**? Did you have an accide**nt**?
B No, nothing like that. My che**st** hur**ts**.

2 **A** It feels like my throat is blo**cked**.
B Should I call an ambula**nce**?

4 SPEAKING

PAIR WORK **Choose a medical problem from this unit. Then follow the instructions below.**

Student A: You have a medical problem. Ask for help and explain what is wrong with you and what happened.

Student B: You see someone who is not well. Ask them about their problem, what happened, and how you can help.

Begin your role plays like this:

A *Are you OK? What's the matter?*

B *I'm not sure, I think ….*

10.4 FACE YOUR FEARS

LESSON OBJECTIVE

- write an email to your future self

1 READING

A PAIR WORK **Decibels (dB) tell us if a sound is loud or quiet. Look at the decibel scale and the list of sounds. Where does each sound go on the scale? Why is *85 dB* red?**

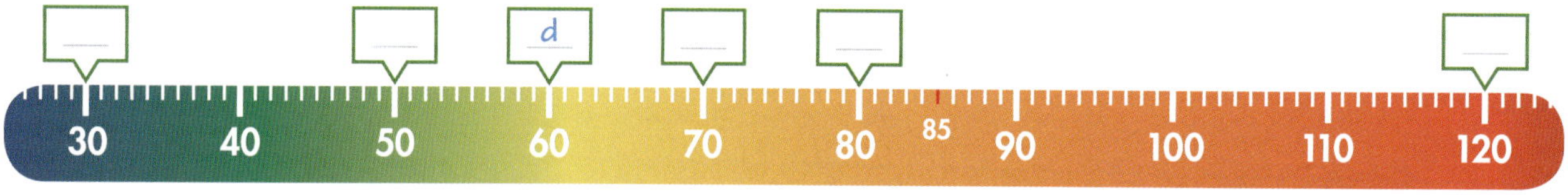

a breathing
b city traffic
c normal conversation
d office noise
e restaurant noise
f rock concert

B PREDICT **Look at the title of the article. Why do you think Janet Horvath is afraid of sound?**

C READ FOR MAIN IDEAS **Read the article and check your answer. How does Janet face her fears?**

A Musician Afraid of Sound

It's 2011 and my husband can't kiss me. The smallest touch hurts me. Everyday noises – a baby crying, the sound of an ATM – are very painful. I'm a professional musician, but I can't stand sound.

It was August 2006. I was a cellist for the Minnesota Orchestra. There were eight speakers on stage. Two of them were too close to my left ear. When I left the stage, I felt a pain in my ears. It went down my neck and into my face. It was terrible. Later, my doctor told me I had a permanent injury from being so close to loud speakers, and my brain was now extremely sensitive to all sound. That meant no TV, no radio, no phone. And, worst of all, no music. It was the worst thing in the world that the thing I loved so much – music – now gave me so much pain.

But I didn't want to give up my career. I loved the cello – it was my life. I had to try to play the cello again.

I had to face my fears. I got a hearing device, and I slowly taught my brain to receive sound again. I can now play with three or four other musicians in a room. I won't be in an orchestra again, but I'll never be without music.

Adapted from an article by musician Janet Horvath in The Atlantic *magazine*

GLOSSARY

sensitive (*adj*) easily affected or damaged by physical activity or effect.
device (*n*) a small machine

D READ FOR DETAILS **Read the article again and find …**

1 Two examples of everyday noises that hurt Janet.
2 Four things she thought she had to live without.
3 One thing (of the four in number 2) that she didn't want to live without.
4 Two things Janet did to play the cello again.

E PAIR WORK THINK CRITICALLY **How many decibels do you think the music from the speakers was? What noisy situations do you experience every day? How many are dangerously high? What can you do to protect your ears from high-decibel sounds?**

2 WRITING

A **Adam is writing an email to himself on a website that will deliver his email to him five years in the future. What is Adam afraid of? What's his advice to himself?**

Reply Forward

To:
From:
Subject: Hello from the past

Hello you! Or really, hello ME, but five years in the future.

It's July 20 and it's 2:03 p.m. I'm 25 years old. When I read this email again, I'll be 30.

I'm writing this email because I want to read about what I was afraid of when I wrote it. And I hope that when I read it in five years, I'll see that everything is OK, that I'm OK.

So, what am I afraid of? I'm afraid of starting a new life in the city. I'm afraid because I don't know anyone, and I'm worried that I won't make any friends, and that I won't be successful in my new career.

I'm leaving a pretty good life. I live with my family in a great apartment. It's home. When I move to the city this fall, where will I live? Who will my friends be? Will I have any friends? Does it all work out well for me? Also, is my hair long, like I want it to be?

Anyway, I really just want to say that I trust you, … me, … us. It's a scary step to take, but it's for the best. You're smart and friendly, you're good at making the best of every situation. Don't be afraid that you made the wrong choice. You have to live your life and take chances! No matter what, it was a good choice.

By the way, you're still looking good. For 30.

Good luck with everything!

Adam (25 years old)

REGISTER CHECK

You're looking good **is a compliment to a friend. To compliment a person older than you, use** ***well*****:**

Hello, Mrs. Garner. ***You're looking well.***

B **WRITING SKILLS** **Look at the phrases in bold in the email. When do you use them? Complete the sentences.**

1 To return to the main idea of what you're saying, use ________________ .

2 To say something new but connected to the main idea, use ________________ .

C **PAIR WORK** **What things are you afraid of? Choose from the word cloud. Compare with a partner. Do you have the same fears?**

I'll be poor. I won't get a good job. I won't have children. I will have children. I will get married. I'll fall in love with the wrong person. My parents won't want me to move away. My children won't be happy. I won't get married. I won't do what I want to do in life.

WRITE IT

D **Think about your answers from exercise 2C and write an email to your future self.**

E **GROUP WORK** **Share your emails. Do people have similar fears?**

10.5

TIME TO SPEAK
Reality TV

LESSON OBJECTIVE
- plan a reality TV show

A What is reality TV? What reality TV shows are most popular at the moment? Do you watch them? Do you like them? Why or why not?

FIND IT

B **RESEARCH** Look at the different kinds of reality TV programs. Think of an example of each. What other types of reality shows do you know? Do you think any of these shows are dangerous? Why or why not? You can use your phone to help you.

C **DISCUSS** Work in small groups. Read the announcement. Brainstorm ideas for a new reality show. Use the questions and the useful phrases below to help you.
- Where will your show be?
- How many people will be on the show? Who will the people be?
- What do the people have to do?
- What "element of danger" will your show have?
- What will make your show exciting to watch?

NEW REALITY SHOW
your ideas wanted!

BIG DEAL PRODUCTIONS, a local TV production company, is accepting ideas for the next big reality show. The show has to have an element of danger, lots of people, and fun situations. Here is your chance to get creative and get on TV!!

D **PREPARE** Prepare a short presentation to the television company producers. Divide your presentation into sections that address the questions in exercise C.

E **PRESENT** Present your show to the producers (the class). Each person in the group should present a part. Then vote on which show is the best in general. Which is the most exciting? Which show is the most dangerous?

To check your progress, go to page 156.

USEFUL PHRASES

DISCUSS
What do you think of … ?
I prefer …
I think we should …

PREPARE
Let's do/choose/think about …
We can talk about …

PRESENT
Our show will be in …
The contestants will have to …
It will be exciting to watch because …

UNIT OBJECTIVES

- talk about what you've done and what you've never done
- talk about what you've done, and when
- make and respond to requests
- write comments about an infographic
- create a video or vlog

ME, ONLINE

11

START SPEAKING

A What can you see in the picture? What are the people doing? Do you do this? Do you like it when other people do this?

B What other types of screens can you add to the list below? How do you use these screens in your life?

ATM computer GPS smartphone tablet TV

C Do you like sharing your photos and videos online? Why or why not? For ideas, watch Irene's video.

REAL STUDENT

Are you the same as Irene?

11.1 I'VE NEVER BEEN HAPPIER!

LESSON OBJECTIVE
- talk about what you've done, and what you've never done

1 LANGUAGE IN CONTEXT

A **Make a list of ten things you want to do in your life. Use the suggestions below, or think of other things.**

buy a car
buy an apartment
find a new job
get married
have a baby
learn to cook
learn to drive
live in a different country
move to a different city
run a marathon
teach someone something
travel to another country
write a book
write a song

B **Read about Elena and her grandmother, Maria. Underline the activities from exercise 1A that they talk about in the interview.**

THIS IS YOUR LIFE

My profile   Sign out

I've **made lots of videos**. But my next video will be my best. It's about my amazing grandmother, Maria Cruz. I interviewed her last week.

Elena Grandma, you've done so many things. You've lived in different places, met interesting people, owned two different businesses, and taught school. What are you most proud of?

Maria Oh, that's easy. I'm most proud of my family. I've watched my children grow up and have beautiful families of their own. I've helped my grandchildren in school, and I've seen two of them graduate from college.

Elena You retired last year, but you haven't slowed down.

Maria No, I haven't. Honestly, the internet has opened up a new world for me. I **check my messages** every day, and I **opened a social media account**. I've **added 200 people as friends** and **joined different groups**. And with my new smartphone, I **message people** all the time.

Elena Have you ever wanted to go back in time, to be young again?

Maria No, I've always loved my life. And now, well, I've never been happier!

C **Read the article again. Who (Elena, Maria, or both of them) … ?**

1 is part of a social network
2 discovered a new world
3 made many videos before now
4 is very proud of her grandchildren

D PAIR WORK **Who is the most interesting person you know? Tell your partner about the person.**

2 VOCABULARY: Using verb–noun internet phrases

A 2.36 **Look at the words in bold in the text and complete the phrases below. Listen and check.**

1 open ____________
2 join ____________
3 make ____________
4 ____________ someone
5 ____________ someone as a friend
6 ____________ your messages

B 2.37 Complete the verb–noun phrases using the words from the box. Listen and check. Were you right?

a website	left or right	on a link	your password

7 build ______________________

8 change ______________________

9 click ______________________

10 swipe ______________________

C Now do the vocabulary exercises for 11.1 on page 151.

D PAIR WORK Do your parents or grandparents use the internet. What do they do? What don't they do? Use the verb-noun phrases from exercise 2.

My grandfather checks his messages once a week. He doesn't want to open a social media account.

3 GRAMMAR: Present perfect for experience

A Circle the correct options to complete the rules. Use the sentences in the grammar box to help you. Underline other examples of the present perfect in the interview on page 108.

1 To make the present perfect, use ***have*** / ***make*** + past participle.
2 For some verbs, the participle is the same as the **simple past** / **present** form.
3 The sentences are about experiences in the **present** / **general past**.
4 To ask if something has happened at any time in the past, use ______________ .
5 To give a negative response, use ______________ in your answer.

Present perfect for experience

I'**ve made** lots of videos.	**Have** you **ever wanted** to go back in time?
I'**ve added** 200 people as friends.	I'**ve never been** happier!

B Now go to page 139. Look at the grammar chart and do the grammar exercise for 11.1.

C Look at the list of activities in exercise 1A on page 108. Which have you done? Which haven't you done? Find the past participle of the verbs. Write five sentences that are true for you. Check your accuracy. Tell your partner. Have you done the same things?

I've learned to drive, but I haven't bought a car.

ACCURACY CHECK

Use *never* + an affirmative verb. Don't use *not* with *never.*

I've ~~not never~~ built a website. ✗
I've never built a website. ✓

4 SPEAKING

GROUP WORK Write a questionnaire with the activities in exercise 1A on page 108. Ask your classmates the questions and write down who has done each thing. Who has done the most things? Who has done the things you want to do?

Have you run a marathon?

Yes, I have.

Great! What's your name?

11.2 SOCIAL MEDIA LIKES

LESSON OBJECTIVE
- talk about what you've done, and when

1 LANGUAGE IN CONTEXT

A PAIR WORK **Answer the questions with a partner.**

A Have you ever crowd-sourced information?
B Have you ever built an app?
C Have you ever made a video that went viral?
D Have you, or anyone you know, ever found love online?

B 2.38 **Listen to three people talk about their online experiences. Which three questions from exercise 1A does the interviewer ask?**

1 Alex ☐ 2 Padma ☐ 3 Sara ☐

C 2.38 PAIR WORK **Listen again. Complete the second question the interviewer asks each person. Check your understanding with a partner.**

2.38 Audio script

1

Alex Not viral really, but my friend and I **uploaded** a video that got about 7,500 views.

Interviewer What ______________________________?

Alex Last year. It was about what music people have on their phones. A guy from the local newspaper even wrote an article about us.

2

Padma I haven't, but my friend has.

Interviewer What ______________________________?

Padma Well, my friend, Ananya, thought she found her cousin Rohan on Facebook. She added him as a friend, but he wasn't her cousin. Same name, different person. She messaged him about the mistake, and he messaged her back, and it continued. Then they decided to meet. They got married last year!

3

Sara Yes, I have.

Interviewer What ______________________________?

Sara We wanted to go to Florida on vacation, but didn't know where to go and what to do. So I put the question out there. I **follow** a photographer from Florida on Instagram, and she messaged me with lots of great travel tips: places to see, really good restaurants, that sort of thing. We got a lot of good suggestions from people, but her advice was the best.

D **Read the answers again. Which person … ?**

1 has a friend whose husband and cousin both have the same name ____________
2 has been in the local newspaper ____________
3 got travel advice from strangers online ____________

2 VOCABULARY: Using social media verbs

FIND IT

A 2.39 **Match the internet icons with the words in the box. You can use your phone to help you. Listen and check.**

block	bookmark	download	follow	go viral
like	log in	search for	share	upload

B **Now do the vocabulary exercises for 11.2 on page 151.**

3 GRAMMAR: Present perfect and simple past

A **Circle the correct options to complete the rules. Use the questions in the grammar box to help you. Then find other examples of the present perfect and simple past in the text in exercise 1B on page 110.**

1 We use the **simple past** / **present perfect** to talk about past experiences not at a specific time.

2 We use the **simple past** / **present perfect** to talk about a specific time in the past.

Present perfect and simple past

Have you **ever made** a video that went viral?
What **was** it about, and when **did** you **make** it?

B **Now go to page 139. Look at the grammar chart and do the grammar exercise for 11.2.**

C PAIR WORK **Write five present perfect sentences about yourself with these verbs. Then give details about each one with the simple past. Tell your partner. Have you done any of the same things?**

eat	lose	break	read	see

4 SPEAKING

A GROUP WORK **Ask your classmates the questions on the right. Make a note of their answers.**

B **Who has been online the most? Who is the biggest user of social media? For ideas, watch Allison's video.**

REAL STUDENT

Did you go online as much as Allison today?

IN THE **LAST WEEK ... ?**

- How many times have you logged in to your social media account?
- How many people have you stopped following on social media?
- Tell me about one comment that you have posted.
- What's the most embarrassing thing you have shared on social media?
- Have you bookmarked anything?

11.3 CAN I USE YOUR PHONE?

LESSON OBJECTIVE

- make and respond to requests

1 FUNCTIONAL LANGUAGE

A 2.40 PAIR WORK **Look at the pictures. What has happened in picture A? What are the people doing in picture B? Read and listen to check.**

A

B

2.40 Audio script

1
A Hello. Can I help you?
B Oh, hi … yes. **Would you mind** looking at my phone?
A **Sure**. What's the problem?
B I dropped it yesterday and broke the screen.
A I can see that!
B So, **can you** fix it?
A **I'm afraid not**. We don't fix screens here.
B Oh, I see. Thanks anyway.

2
A This is so beautiful. Let's take a selfie.
B Smile! Oh, no!
A What's wrong?
B My phone. The battery's dead. **Do you mind if I** use yours?
A **No problem**.
B Thanks. OK … Smile! … Perfect. Actually, **could I** take a few more?
A **Yeah, that's fine**. I can share them with you later.
B Great. Thanks so much.

B **Complete the chart with expressions in bold from the conversations above.**

Making requests	Responding to requests
Asking someone to do something	**Accepting**
Would you [1] ______ (looking at my phone)?	Sure.
[2] ______ / Could you (fix it)?	No [5] ______.
	Yeah, that's [6] ______.
Asking for permission	**Refusing**
Do you mind [3] ______ I (use your phone)?	I'm [7] ______ not.
Can / [4] ______ I (take a few more)?	No, I'm sorry.

INSIDER ENGLISH

When a phone battery has no power, you can say that it's *dead*.

*The battery is **dead**.*

*My phone **died**.*

C PAIR WORK **Practice the conversations in exercise 1A with a partner.**

2 REAL-WORLD STRATEGY

A 2.41 **Listen to a conversation in a repair shop. What's the problem?**

B 2.41 **Read the information in the box about remembering words. Then listen to the conversation again. What question from the box does the customer use?**

> **REMEMBERING WORDS**
>
> When you can't remember a word, someone's name, or don't know how to say something in English, you can ask a question:
>
> *What's his/her name?* *What do you call it/them?*

C 2.42 **Complete another conversation with a question from the box. Listen and check.**

A I uploaded a photo of that actor I saw.

B Who?

A You know, ______________________? The really good one. She won an award last year.

B Oh, yeah. With all the hair. I know who you mean. What *is* her name?

D **Student A: Go to page 158. Student B: Go to page 160. Follow the instructions.**

3 PRONUNCIATION: Saying final /n/ and /m/ sounds

A 2.43 **Listen to the words. Focus on the sound of the bold letters. Practice saying them. Do you make the /n/ and /m/ sounds?**

/n/ pho**n**e broke**n** wo**n** /m/ proble**m** progra**m** na**m**e

B 2.44 **Circle the words that end in the /m/ sound. Listen and check. Practice the conversations with a partner. Is your mouth open or closed when you say the /m/ sound?**

1 **A** What's the problem?
B My phone is broken. Can you fix it?
A I'm afraid not.

2 **A** What's his name?
B It's Robin.

3 **A** It's warm in here.
B The windows are closed.
A Do you mind if I open them?
B That's fine.

4 SPEAKING

PAIR WORK **Choose <u>two</u> of the situations. Practice making and responding to requests. You can accept or refuse each request.**

1 You're a tourist. Ask someone to take your picture.
2 You're in an office or on a bus, and it's very hot. Check if it's OK to open the window.
3 You're having a problem buying a soda from a machine. Another person is waiting.
4 You're in a hurry to a buy a train ticket. You want to go to the front of the line.

Would you mind taking a photo of us?

Sure. No problem.

Thanks a lot. Just press here.

11.4 SELFIES

LESSON OBJECTIVE

- write comments about an infographic

1 READING

A PAIR WORK **How often do you take selfies? Find a selfie that you love or hate. Talk about where, when, and how you took the picture.**

B READ FOR MAIN IDEAS **Read the blog page. Check (✓) the topics that the writer includes.**

1 how often people take selfies ☐
2 problems with selfies (selfie fails!) ☐
3 selfies and social media ☐
4 famous people's selfies ☐
5 the age of people who take selfies ☐
6 how to take a good selfie ☐
7 why people take selfies ☐
8 where people take selfies ☐

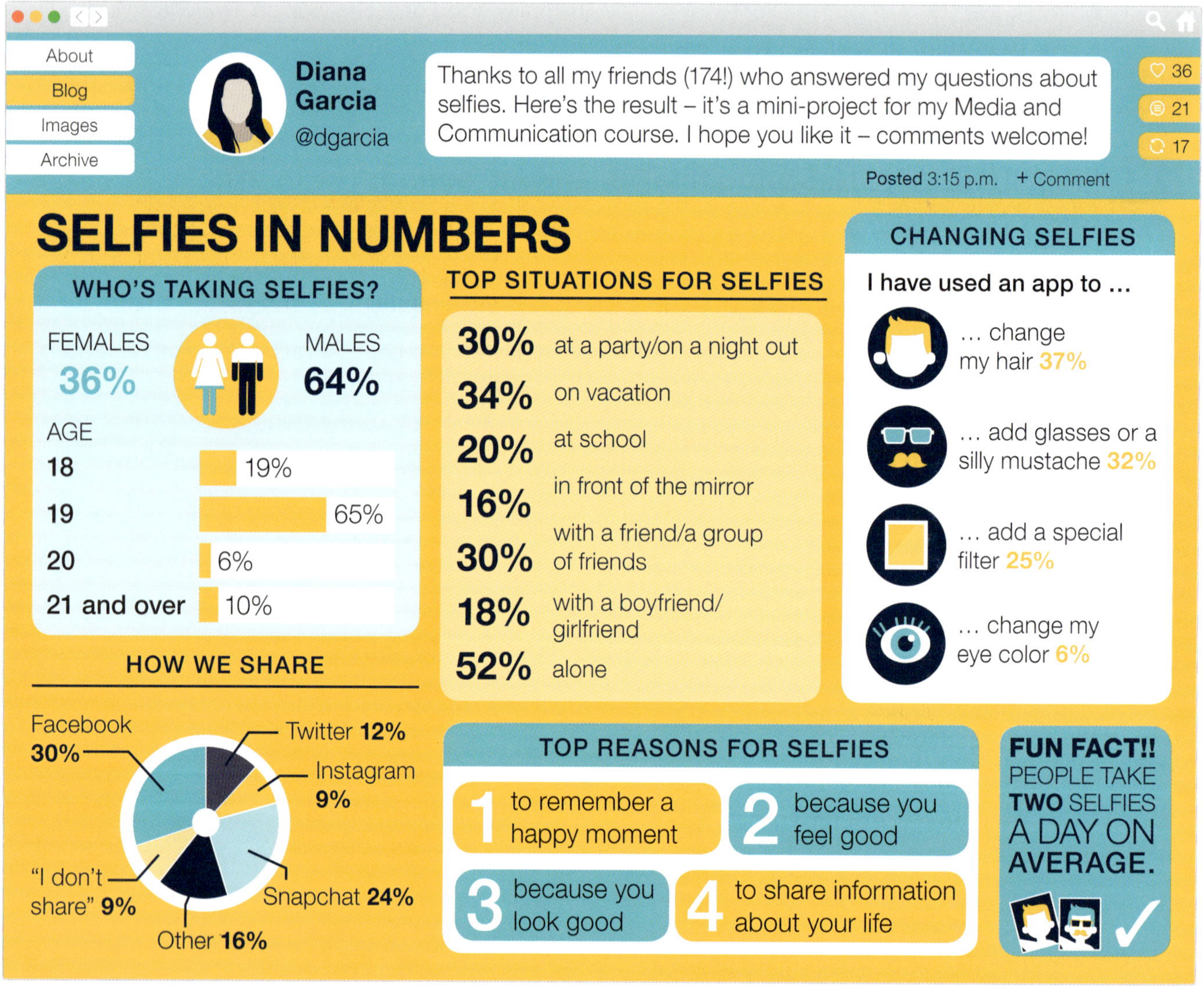

C READ FOR DETAIL **Read the blog again. Which sentences are true? Correct the false ones.**

1 Teenagers take the most selfies.
2 Parties are the most popular place for selfies.
3 People take selfies with friends the most.
4 People often take selfies when they're happy.
5 Most people share their selfies on social media.
6 Apps are popular for changing eye color.

D PAIR WORK THINK CRITICALLY **Choose the statement that best summarizes Diana's infographic about selfies. Discuss your ideas with a partner.**

A People take them because they are lonely.
B They're about sharing positive experiences.
C They're not fashionable now.
D They're a good way to make friends.

2 WRITING

A **Look at the comments about Diana's infographic. Which are positive, and which are negative?**

COMMENTS (3)
SELFIES IN NUMBERS

Maia-gio

I loved this infographic! It's so good to see what real people say about selfies. I think it's interesting that so many of us take selfies when we are alone – 52%! I also can't believe that more men than women take selfies! Are you sure? 😂

Victor Victor

I take selfies all the time, but I've never stopped to think about them. This infographic has so much interesting information. I always thought people just took selfies when they looked good. I was surprised that the top reasons were when they feel good or happy!

Tim Popa

This infographic is such a waste of time. 32% add a silly mustache! 16% take selfies in front of the mirror! Who cares? Can we have some real information, please? 😒

REGISTER CHECK

Who cares? (informal) = *it isn't useful or important.*

B WRITING SKILLS **Look at the phrases in the box. Match them to their uses. Find more examples in the comments in exercise A.**

I always thought …	I think it's interesting that …	Who cares?

1 to say something positive: ____________
2 to say something negative: ____________
3 to say that you had a different idea before: ____________

C PAIR WORK **Look at the infographic on page 114 again. Which information do you think is most interesting? Which information is not interesting? Why?**

WRITE IT

D **Use your answers in exercise 2C to help you write a short comment of about 50 words. You can:**

- say what you like or don't like about the infographic
- ask a question about the information
- use emojis, like these: 😂 😒

E PAIR WORK **Show your comment to a partner. Write a reply to your partner's comment.**

11.5 TIME TO SPEAK
Online videos

LESSON OBJECTIVE
- create a video or vlog

A **Look at the types of videos on sites like YouTube. Which ones have you watched? Do you know any others? Add them to the list.**

- music videos
- beauty and fashion advice
- "how-to" videos
- cute animal videos
- food or travel vlogs
- ______
- ______
- ______

B **RESEARCH** **Think of a famous YouTuber. What do they make videos about? Can you describe them to the class? Why do you think they are popular?**

C **DISCUSS** **Imagine you're going to make a video. What is it going to be about? Think of something you want to tell people, for example:**

- something you have done
- somewhere you have been
- something you are interested in
- something you know how to do

D **PREPARE** **In small groups, you are going to make a video. Plan what you are going to say and do in the video. Use the phrases at the bottom of the page to help you. Think about the following questions:**

- What type of video will you make?
- What will it be about?
- Who will star in your video? What will they say?
- What will happen in your video?
- Who will film and direct the video?

E **PRESENT** **Show your video to your classmates, and watch their videos. What do you like about each video? Do you think there are any future YouTube celebrities in your class?**

To check your progress, go to page 156.

USEFUL PHRASES

DISCUSS
Have you heard of … ?
I really like watching his/her/their videos because …

PREPARE
I have a good idea.
I think we should …
How about … ?

PRESENT
This is our video.
That's really cool/funny/interesting.
You've done a really good job!
I think you'll be famous one day!

UNIT OBJECTIVES

- talk about the weather
- describe places, people, and things
- ask for and give directions
- write simple instructions
- create a tourism campaign for your country

OUTDOORS

12

START SPEAKING

A Look at the picture. What's happening? What time of year do you think it is? Why? Think of three causes for wildfires like this one.

B Do you ever have big fires in your country? Where and when do they usually happen? Have you ever seen a big fire?

C Does it get very hot or very cold in your country? Which do you prefer, hot weather or cold weather? Why? For ideas, watch Allison's video.

Do you agree with Allison?

12.1 NINE MONTHS, EIGHT COUNTRIES

LESSON OBJECTIVE
- talk about the weather

1 VOCABULARY: Describing weather

DARK / WET	**COLD**	**HOT**	**STORMY**	**EXTREME**
cloudy	freezing	boiling	blizzard	drought
foggy	snowy	sunny	snowstorm	flood
humid			thunder and lightning	hurricane
rainy			windy	

A 2.45 **Listen and repeat the weather words. Can you think of more words for each category?**

B **Look at the list of weather words again. Which are adjectives? Underline them. Which are nouns? Circle them.**

C **Now do the vocabulary exercises for 12.1 on page 152.**

D PAIR WORK **How would you describe your local weather for different seasons?**

> **!** For temperatures, we use "degrees."
> *24° C = 24* ***degrees*** *Celsius*
> *65° F = 65* ***degrees*** *Fahrenheit*

2 LANGUAGE IN CONTEXT

A 2.46 **Listen to the introduction to a radio interview. Who is Jonathan Brookner? Why is he in the studio?**

B 2.47 **Think of three questions you want to ask Jonathan about his trip. Then listen to the interview. Did the interviewer ask the same questions?**

2.47 Audio script

Host Jonathan, tell us some more about your adventures. What was the weather like in all these places?

Jonathan We experienced every kind of weather possible! In Patagonia, we were in a **snowstorm** that lasted for three days. It was **freezing** and so **windy**!

Host That's a long time to be in the middle of a snowstorm!

Jonathan In Ecuador it was worse! There was a huge tropical storm, with really heavy rain and **thunder and lightning**. There were **floods**, and the roads were closed. We stayed there for a few days to help the local people clean up the mess.

Host Did you get any good weather?

Jonathan Uruguay had good weather. It was perfect: warm and **sunny**.

Host Thanks Jonathan, let's take another short break, we'll be back in two minutes …

C 2.47 **Read and listen again. Answer the questions.**

1 What weather did Jonathan enjoy most?

2 What weather did he enjoy least?

3 What extreme weather did they experience?

D PAIR WORK **What's your favorite kind of weather? What is your least favorite kind of weather? Why? Where and when have you experienced each of them?**

3 GRAMMAR: *be like*

A **Complete the rules. Use the sentences in the grammar box to help you.**

1 Use the verb ______________ + *like* to ask questions about things.

2 Answer these questions with **verbs / adjectives**.

> ***be like***
>
> What **was** the weather **like**?
>
> It **was** freezing and so windy.

B **Draw lines to match the questions (1–3) and answers (a–c).**

1 What's the weather like?

2 What was the party like?

3 What will the course be like?

a It'll be hard work!

b It's cold and windy.

c It was great! We had a really good time.

C **Now go to page 140. Look at the grammar chart and do the grammar exercise for 12.1.**

D PAIR WORK **Think about a person you've known for a long time. Ask and answer the questions. Check your accuracy. Then tell your partner.**

1 What was he/she like when he/she was younger?

2 Is he/she very different now? What is he/she like today?

> **ACCURACY CHECK**
>
> **When you are answering a question with *what … like?* don't use *like* with adjectives in the answer.**
>
> *What was the weather like?*
>
> It was ~~like~~ cold and windy. ✗
>
> It was cold and windy. ✓

4 SPEAKING

A GROUP WORK **Think of a city you know well. Answer the questions.**

- What's the weather like in your city today? What's it going to be like next weekend?
- What's the weather usually like in December? In July?
- Does the city have good weather in general?

B **Tell the class your answers to the questions in exercise 4A with more details.**

12.2 THIS TRIP HAS IT ALL

LESSON OBJECTIVE
- describe places, people, and things

1 VOCABULARY: Describing landscapes and cityscapes

A **Look at the pictures. What do you think the weather is like in each place? Which picture do you like the most? Why?**

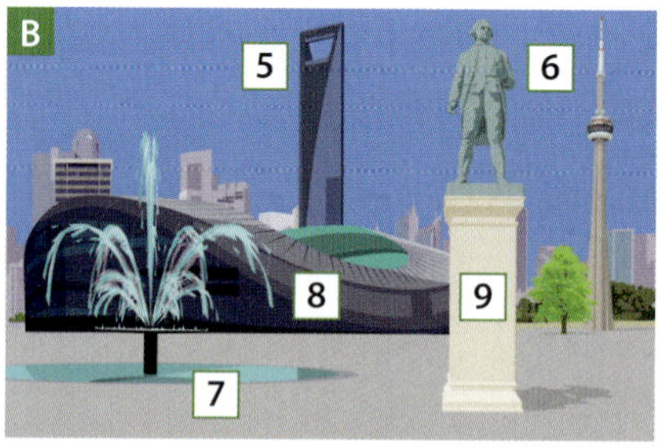

B 2.48 **Which features from the box can you usually find in the city? In nature? Listen and repeat. Then label the pictures with what you can see.**

☐ cave	☐ cliff	☐ coast	☐ fountain	☐ glacier
1 rainforest	☐ rocks	☐ skyscraper	☐ stadium	☐ statue
☐ stream	☐ tower	☐ valley	☐ waterfall	

C **Now do the vocabulary exercises for 12.2 on page 152.**

D PAIR WORK **Think of the landscape around your town. What's it like? Which landscape features can you find near you? Which cityscape features can you find near you?**

2 LANGUAGE IN CONTEXT

A PAIR WORK **When you travel, do you prefer to go to the coast, the mountains, or the city? Why?**

B **Read about a trip to Ecuador. Would you like to take this trip?**

EIGHT DAYS IN ECUADOR

Day by day | Dates and prices | Accommodation

From the skyscrapers of Quito to the rocky cliffs of the Galapagos Islands, this trip has it all! Everyone who takes this trip falls in love with our beautiful country.

DAY 1

You'll take a guided tour around Quito. We have tour guides that speak English and Spanish. If you'd like a tour in another language, just ask! The tour will end at the top of El Panecillo Hill, where you can see the famous Virgen de Quito **statue** and take photos of the amazing views of the city and the mountains all around it.

DAY 2

You will leave the busy city and take a plane to Baltra in the Galapagos Islands. You'll get on a boat which goes to the Charles Darwin Research Station. You can learn about the strange animals that live on the islands and the interesting trees and flowers that grow there. You can even see some of the giant tortoises walking around on the **rocks**.

DAY 3

...

C **Read the information again. What can you do in Quito? What can you do in the Galapagos Islands?**

D PAIR WORK Are there different landscapes in your country? How many different kinds can you name? Describe them. Which one do you like the most? Why? For ideas, watch Seung Geyoung's video.

Is your favorite place like Seung Geyoung's?

3 GRAMMAR: Relative pronouns: *who, which, that*

A **Circle the correct options to complete the rules. Use the sentences in the grammar box to help you.**

1 Use ***who/which*** and *that* for people.

2 Use ***who/which*** and *that* for things.

Relative pronouns: *who, which, that*

Everyone **who** takes this trip falls in love with our beautiful country.
We have our tour guides **that** speak English and Spanish.
You'll get on a boat **which** goes to the Charles Darwin Research Station.
You can learn about the strange animals **that** live there.

B **Now go to page 140. Look at the grammar chart and do the grammar exercise for 12.2 .**

! **You can use *that* for both people and things.**

*That's the man **that** we met in Quito. Remember? He's wearing the hat **that** he bought at the market there.*

4 SPEAKING

A **Complete the descriptions using *who*, *which*, or *that*.**
Then think of a person, object, or place for each of the descriptions.

1 the person ______________ helped me most at school ______________

2 a song ______________ reminds me of summer ______________

3 a landscape ______________ makes me feel relaxed ______________

4 the people ______________ I spend the most time with ______________

5 one thing ______________ I would really like to do in the future ______________

B PAIR WORK **Tell your partner about your answers in exercise 4A.**

12.3 I THINK WE'RE LOST

LESSON OBJECTIVE
- ask for and give directions

1 FUNCTIONAL LANGUAGE

A **2.49** **Have you ever gotten lost? Where were you? Did you ask for help? Read and listen to the conversations. Where do the people want to go?**

2.49 Audio script

1 A Hello, **excuse me, we're looking for the waterfall. Are we going in the right direction**?
B The waterfall? No, **you need to go back the way you came.**
A Oh. That's a long way.
B See that hill there?
A The one with the tall tree on top?
B **Yes, turn right after that hill. Walk for a couple of miles, and you'll see the waterfall on the left.**
A Thanks. I hope this is a really beautiful waterfall.

2 A **Excuse me, can you help us, please**? **We're lost**, and my phone just died.
B Yeah, sure. Where do you want to go?
A Well, **we need to get to** the nearest subway station.
B OK, let me look at my phone . . . . Yeah, **at the next intersection turn right. Walk three blocks** to King Street **and then turn left**. You'll see the park ahead of you. **The subway station's right there.**
A That's great. Thanks!
B Keep walking toward the park and you can't miss it!

INSIDER ENGLISH

People often say *you can't miss it* when a place is really easy to find.

B Complete the chart with expressions in **bold** from the conversations above.

Asking for directions	Giving directions
Excuse me, we're [1] ___ for (the waterfall). Are we going in the [2] ___ direction? Excuse me, [3] ___ ___ us, please? We're [4] ___ .	You need to [5] ___ ___ the way you came. [6] ___ right (after the hill). Walk for (a couple of miles), and you'll see (the waterfall) [7] ___ ___ ___ . At the next intersection [8] ___ right. Walk (three) [9] ___ and then turn left. The (subway station's) right [10] ___ .

C PAIR WORK Practice the conversations in exercise 1A with your partner.

2 REAL-WORLD STRATEGY

A 2.50 Listen to the conversation. Where does the woman want to go?

B 2.50 Read the information about correcting yourself in the box below. Listen to the conversation again. How many times does the man correct himself with the phrases from the box?

CORRECTING YOURSELF

When you've given incorrect information, you can correct yourself with these phrases:

Well, actually … *No, wait …*

C PAIR WORK Write three sentences about you. Give a wrong detail in each sentence. Then tell a partner your sentence, and correct the information.

3 PRONUNCIATION: Saying /w/ at the beginning of a word

A 2.51 Listen. Focus on the sound of the letters in **bold**. Practice saying them. Do you make the /w/ sound?

Excuse me, **w**e're looking for the **w**aterfall.

B 2.52 Listen. Which speaker, A or B, says the /w/ sound?

A **W**here are you and your **w**ife **w**alking to?

B **W**e're **w**alking to the **w**aterfall.

A **W**ait, this isn't the **w**ay to the **w**aterfall!

B **W**ell, actually, **w**e **w**ant to **w**alk through the **w**oods first because the **w**eather's so **w**indy.

C PAIR WORK Practice the conversation in exercise 3B. Focus on the /w/ sounds. Look at the conversations in exercise 1A on page 122. Find more examples of words with the /w/ sound at the beginning.

4 SPEAKING

FIND IT

A PAIR WORK Think about special places in your town. Take turns asking for and giving directions to those places from where you are now. Remember to check that you understand the directions. You can use the map on your phone.

B Were your directions accurate, or did you have to correct yourself? Whose directions were the easiest to follow?

12.4 GUERRILLA GARDENING

LESSON OBJECTIVE
- write simple instructions

1 LISTENING

A PREDICT **Look at the pictures. Where are the people? What are they doing? Why do you think they're doing it at night?**

B 2.53 LISTEN FOR SPECIFIC INFORMATION **Listen to Bruna Andreotti talking about guerrilla gardening. Check your predictions in exercise 1A.**

C 2.53 LISTEN FOR DETAILS **Listen again. Complete the sentences.**

1 A guerrilla gardener is a person who ______________.
2 They plant things on land that ______________.
3 They do it to make their neighborhoods ______________.
4 Bruna's group runs a community garden that ______________.

D PAIR WORK THINK CRITICALLY **Do you think guerrilla gardens are a good idea for improving city neighborhoods? Why or why not? What other solutions are there?**

E **Which places would be good for a guerrilla gardening project in your city? Would you like to be part of a project like this? Why or why not?**

2 PRONUNCIATION: Listening for *t* when it sounds like *d*

A 2.54 **Listen. Focus on the bold letters. What letter do they sound like?**

1 in the middle of a ci**t**y
2 People throw less li**tt**er.
3 They si**t** outside on the street.

B 2.55 **Circle the letter *t* when it changes to sound like *d*. What sounds are before and after it? Listen and check.**

1 a really positive effect
2 We also have a community garden.
3 It's about working together to do something good for our city and our community.

C **Complete the sentence.**

The letter *t* is often pronounced like ___ when it is between two ______________ sounds.

3 WRITING

A Read these instructions for how to be a guerrilla gardener. Would you add any steps?

HOW TO ... be a guerrilla gardener

Here are five simple steps to get started as a guerrilla gardener. *Anyone can do it!*

First, choose a place in your neighborhood that nobody uses or cares about.

Then, decide what kinds of plants you want to plant. Flowers? Fruit? Vegetables?

Next, go to a gardening center and choose your plants. Also, buy any tools you might need.

Now go out at a quiet time and plant your plants.

Finally, water your plants and watch them grow!

B **WRITING SKILLS** **Read the text again and find the sequence words in the box. Complete the sentences below.**

finally	first	next	now	then

1 Use ______________ to introduce the starting point.

2 Use ______________, ______________, and ______________ to show the order of other points.

3 Use ______________ to make the last point.

C **You're going to write a short how-to text like the one in exercise 3A. Decide what you're going to write about. Use one of the ideas here or your own idea.**

Five simple steps to ...

- making spaghetti
- dancing salsa
- choosing a pet
- learning new vocabulary

WRITE IT

D **Decide on the five steps. Read the text in exercise 3A again and <u>underline</u> any phrases you can use. Then write your text. Keep your text short and simple, and remember to use sequence words.**

E **PAIR WORK** **Read some of your classmates' texts. Which are the easiest instructions to follow? Can you remember the instructions? Tell your partner.**

12.5 TIME TO SPEAK
Places that you'll love

LESSON OBJECTIVE
- create a tourism campaign for your country

A **DISCUSS** **Look at the three pictures. What can you see in each one? Which place would you most like to visit? Why? Are there similar places near you?**

Tofino Beach

Lake Monroe

The Rockies

B **All three pictures are from the same country. What country do you think it is? Why?**

C **Read the announcement. Discuss the questions to help think of ideas for your entry.**
- What different kinds of landscapes are in your country? Make a list of places that are very interesting and/or beautiful.
- Which places in your country are famous? Why are they famous?
- Which places are the most popular with visitors? Are there any special places that most tourists don't know about? Where are they? Why are they special?
- What's the weather like in different seasons? When is the best time of year to visit?

> COME TO OUR
> # COUNTRY!
>
> **The Tourism Office needs your help with a program to attract tourists to our beautiful country.**
>
> **PLACES:** Send us information about three spectacular places in our country that you think should be on our tourism site. Explain why you think each one is special, and suggest photos for each of the three places.
>
> **SLOGANS:** Send us your ideas for a phrase or sentence to get people's attention and make them want to know more about our country.
>
> *Submissions are due by **September 21**.*

D **PREPARE** **Work with a partner and prepare an entry for your country. Use the phrases at the bottom of the page to help you.**
- Choose three places which you think tourists would like. What are they like? What can you do there?
- Write your reasons for choosing each place.
- Think of at least one slogan for the tourism campaign.
- Write a description of the three photos you want to include with your entry. Go online to find some examples if you want.

FIND IT

E **PRESENT** **Present your entry to the class. Listen to the other presentations, and decide which places you want to go to and why. Which campaign had the best slogan?**

To check your progress, go to page 156.

USEFUL PHRASES

DISCUSS
I'd really like to go there because …
It looks exciting / pretty / amazing.
It's similar to where I live.

PREPARE
Where do you want to talk about?
Have you ever been to … ? / Do you know … well?

PRESENT
We think tourists would love … because …
This place is really special to me because …

REVIEW 4 (UNITS 10–12)

1 VOCABULARY

A **Put the words in the box into the correct categories.**

accountant	ankle	architect	block	cliff	coast	fever
follow	freezing	humid	hurricane	mechanic	neck	nurse
search	share	stomachache	stream	thunder	valley	waterfall

Jobs: ______________________________

Health and body: ______________________________

The internet: ______________________________

Weather: ______________________________

Landscapes: ______________________________

B PAIR WORK **Think of one more word from each category. Add them to the lists in exercise 1A. Compare with a partner. Did you write the same words?**

2 GRAMMAR

A **Circle the correct options to complete the conversations.**

1 **A** You [1]*'ve been / went* to a glacier, haven't you? What [2]*are they / was it* like?
  B Yes, I [3]*have / am*. It was freezing!

2 **A** How do I block these ads [4]*that / who* appear on my screen all the time?
  B It's easy. You [5]*don't have to / have to* download anything. Just click there.

3 **A** What's the weather [6]*going to be like / going to like* at the coast?
  B A friend [7]*has told / told* me yesterday that it [8]*might be / might being* rainy.

B PAIR WORK **Complete the sentences so that they are true for you. Compare them with a partner.**

1 I've never been to … .
  I've never been to Europe, but I'd love to go one day.
2 I have a friend who … .
3 Every week I have to … .
4 Tomorrow morning I think I might … .
5 Last week I bought something that … .

3 SPEAKING

A PAIR WORK **Think of a beautiful place in your country that you have been to. Follow the instructions for the conversation.**

1 Ask your partner if he/she has ever been to that place.
2 Exchange opinions using questions with *what … like*.
3 Talk about the best things that people can see or do there.
4 Invite your partner to come to that place with you sometime soon. Use *have to* and *don't have to* to encourage your partner to come.

4 FUNCTIONAL LANGUAGE

A **Complete the conversation at a basketball game.**

can I could you hurts no problem sure what happened? you mind

A Are you OK? [1] ______________

B I twisted my ankle. It really [2] ______________ .

A How [3] ______________ help?

B [4] ______________ get a chair for me, please? And maybe some ice?

A [5] ______________ , just a second … Here you go. Do you think we should call an ambulance?

B No, I don't think that's necessary. But would [6] ______________ getting me a taxi?

A [7] ______________ . I'll call for one right now.

B Thank you!

B PAIR WORK **Practice reading the conversation in pairs.**

C **Read the directions. Where do you get to from where you are now?**

1 Turn left as you go out of the door. At the next intersection, turn right. Walk for three blocks.

2 Turn right at the door. Walk for four blocks. Cross the street and take the first left.

D **Where is the nearest grocery store? Write down some more directions and read them to your partner. Were your directions the same as your partner's?**

5 SPEAKING

A PAIR WORK **Choose one of the situations. Act it out in pairs.**

1 You have a bad toothache. Go to the drugstore. Explain your problem and ask for advice.

A Hello, can I help you?

B Yes, please. I have a horrible toothache …

2 You have broken the screen on your phone. Go to a phone shop and ask them to replace the screen. Ask about the price and the time it will take.

A Hello, can you help me?

B I can try. What's the problem?

3 Some tourists stop you outside the school. They are lost. They want directions to the nearest subway or bus stop. Help them.

A Excuse me, can you help us? We're lost.

B Sure. Where do you want to go?

B **Change roles and repeat the role play.**

GRAMMAR REFERENCE AND PRACTICE

1.1 *BE*; POSSESSIVE ADJECTIVES (page 3)

be

	Affirmative	Negative	Question	Short answers
I	**am** from Indiana.	**'m not** from Florida.	**Am** I late?	Yes, I **am**. No, I**'m not**.
He / She / It	**is** my roommate.	**'s not** my boyfriend.	**Is** he/she/it from Indiana?	Yes, he **is**. No, he **isn't**.
You / We / They	**are** close friends.	**'re not** close friends.	**Are** they your neighbors?	Yes, they **are**. No, they're **not**.

A **Complete the sentences with the correct verb or possessive adjective. Use contractions where possible.**

1 We're ________ students. ________ names are Marc and Belinda.

2 He ________ from Scotland. ________ name is Ron.

3 I ________ Colombian, but ________ mother is from Brazil.

4 They ________ in the classroom. ________ teacher is Emily.

5 ________ name is Mr. Brinkley. He ________ the boss.

6 My city ________ famous for ________ tacos.

! People usually say:	You can also say:
*you**'re not***	*you **aren't***
*we**'re not***	*we **aren't***
*they**'re not***	*he/she/**it isn't***
*he**'s**/she**'s**/it**'s not***	*he/she/**it isn't***

1.2 POSSESSION (page 5)

Possession (pages 3 and 5)

Subject pronouns	Possessive adjectives		Possessive pronouns	
I	**my**	It's **my** mirror.	**mine**	It's **mine**.
you	**your**	It's **your** bottle.	**yours**	It's **yours**.
he	**his**	It's **his** brush.	**his**	It's **his**.
she	**her**	It's **her** gum.	**hers**	It's **hers**.
we	**our**	It's **our** house.	**ours**	It's **ours**.
they	**their**	It's **their** umbrella.	**theirs**	It's **theirs**.
Use *whose* to ask about possession. *__Whose__ is this? __Whose__ bag is this? It's mine.* We can also say ***Who** does this (bag) **belong to**? It's mine. / It belongs to me.*				
***'s* shows possession** my son**'s** keychain (= the keychain that belongs to my son)				

A **Circle the correct options to complete the conversations.**

1 **A** *Who's* / *Whose* car is that?
B It's not *our* / *ours*.

2 **A** *Who* / *Whose* does this cash belong to? Is it *your* / *yours*?
B No. It's *mine* / *my sister's*.

3 **A** Whose hairbrush *is this* / *does this belong to*?
B It's *my mother's* / *of my mother*.

4 **A** Hey! That's *mine* / *my*.
B No, it isn't. It *belongs* / *is* to me.

5 **A** Is this *your* / *yours* umbrella?
B No, it's *Donna* / *Donna's*. *Mine* / *My* is red.

> **!**
> ***Who's* = Who is**
> ***Who's*** *from Puebla? Cecilia.*
> ***Whose* = possession**
> ***Whose family*** *lives in Puebla? Cecilia's.*

2.1 SIMPLE PRESENT FOR HABITS AND ROUTINES (page 13)

Simple present for habits and routines

	Affirmative	Negative	Question	Short answers
I	**sleep** for eight hours.	**don't sleep** much.		
He / She / It	**sleeps** for six hours.	**doesn't sleep** much.	**Does** she **sleep** a lot?	Yes, she **does**. No, he **doesn't**.
You / We / They	**sleep** for seven hours.	**don't sleep** much.	**Do** you **sleep** a lot?	Yes, we **do**. No, they **don't**.

Information questions
Where does he **study**?
Why do we **have** homework?
How do they **get** to and from work? **How many** hours **do** you **sleep** a night?

Time phrases
Every day/evening/week/month
On Monday/the weekend
In the morning/the afternoon/the evening

A **Use the words to write simple present sentences.**

1 **A** What time / your daughter / get up / on the weekend?
What time does your daughter get up on the weekend?
B She / usually / get up / very late.
____

2 **A** How often / you / ride to work / together?
____
B We / always / ride to work together, / but / Laura / not drive.
____

3 **A** How often / watch TV / on the weekend?
____
B I / not / watch TV / on the weekend. I / watch TV / every evening after work.
____

2.2 *THIS / THAT ONE; THESE / THOSE ONES* (page 15)

A **Circle the correct words to complete the sentences. Then match the questions (1–6) and the answers (a–f).**

1 Is *these / this / those* your coffee? ___
2 Can I use *that / these / those* outlet, please? ___
3 *That / This / Those* headphones don't work. ___
4 Are *that / this / those* your notes? ___
5 What's *that / these / this* over there? ___
6 How much does *that / these / those* phone cost? ___

a That *one / ones* costs $245.
b Then use these *one / ones*.
c Yes, they are.
d No, that *one / ones* is my coffee.
e No, please use that *one / ones*.
f I don't know what *that / these / those* is.

3.1 PRESENT CONTINUOUS (page 23)

Present continuous

	Affirmative	Negative	Question	Short answers
I	**'m winning**.	**'m not watching** the game.		
You / We / They	**'re going** to the gym.	**'re not playing** well.	**Are** they **winning**?	Yes, they **are**. No, they **aren't**.
He / She / It	**'s losing**.	**'s not having** a good game.	**Is** it **raining**?	Yes, it **is**. No, it **isn't**.

A **Complete the live-feed events with the present continuous of the verbs in parentheses.**

SPORTS LIVE

The swimmers [1] ___*are coming*___ (come) in now. They [2] ______ (wait) for the start. The champion [3] ______ (look) at the fans, but she [4] ______ (not smile). She has her headphones on – what music [5] ______ (she listen) to?

B **Use the words to write sentences. Use the present continuous of the verbs.**

1 The people / leave / the stadium ______
2 The drivers / start / their engines ______
3 What / the coach / do? ______
4 It / rain / but / the runners / not stop ______
5 The winner / smile / and / cry ______
6 My favorite player / not win / any games at the moment ______
7 He / run / with the ball ______
8 The fans / wear / team hats ______

3.2 SIMPLE PRESENT AND PRESENT CONTINUOUS (page 25)

A **Read the conversations. Complete the sentences with the simple present or present continuous of the verbs in parentheses.**

1 **A** What ______________________ (you / do)?
  B I'm waiting for my friend.

2 **A** Does he go to a gym?
  B Yes, ______________________ (do).

3 **A** Can you talk now?
  B No, I can't. I ______________________ (drive).

4 **A** You ______________________ (not / listen) to me!
  B Sorry, I ______________________ (watch) the game.

5 **A** What ______________________ (you / read)?
  B It's a book about exercise.

6 **A** Mom! Ben ______________________ (kick) me again!
  B Stop it, Ben!

7 **A** Why ______________________ (you / lie down)?
  B Because I'm tired.

8 **A** Hurry! The game starts in two minutes.
  B I ______________________ (come)!

4.1 PRESENT CONTINUOUS FOR FUTURE PLANS (page 35)

Present continuous for future plans			
Affirmative	**Negative**	**Question**	**Information question**
Comic Con **is coming** here this weekend.	He **isn't selling** anything.	**Are** you **going** to Comic Con?	What **are** you **doing** later?

A **Use the words to write sentences about future plans. Use contractions when you can.**

> **!** **Present continuous for plans usually includes a future time expression.**
> *What are you doing* ***tomorrow****?*
> *We're going to the beach* ***on the weekend****.*

1 My cousin / play in a concert / next Saturday.
  My cousin's playing in a concert next Saturday.

2 I / go to a concert / with my best friend tonight.
  ____

3 you / play video games / with your friends later?
  ____

4 We / watch our team / at the stadium on my birthday.
  ____

5 We / not go / to the pool today.
  ____

6 She / not go to the game / this weekend.
  ____

4.2 OBJECT PRONOUNS (page 37)

Subject pronoun	Object pronoun	
I / we	me / us	They buy great gifts for **me** / **us**.
you	you	I'm getting a special gift for **you**.
he / she / they	him / her / them	I'm seeing **him** / **her** / **them** tomorrow.
it	it	This is a great gift! I love **it**!

A **Circle the correct options to complete the conversations.**

1 **A** We're having a party on Saturday. Do you think John would like to come?
B Why don't you ask *her / him / me*?

2 **A** My grandparents are visiting us right now.
B Oh yeah? Please say hello to *him / us / them* for me!

3 **A** Is your brother coming to my party this weekend?
B Yes, he is. And he's bringing a special gift for *him / it / you*.

4 **A** Do you like soccer?
B Do I like soccer? I love *them / you / it*!

5 **A** My mom is starting a new job next week.
B Really? Tell *her / him / you* good luck!

6 **A** Can I ask *her / us / you* a question?
B Yeah, sure thing. What do you want to ask?

5.1 SIMPLE PAST (page 45)

Simple past of *be*

	Affirmative	Negative	Question	Short answers
I / He / She / It	**was** cool.	**wasn't** loud.	**Was** it fun?	Yes, it **was**. / No, it **wasn't**.
You / We / They	**were** perfect.	**weren't** proud.	**Were** they crazy?	Yes, they **were**. / No, they **weren't**.

Simple past

Regular verbs: verb + -(*e*)*d*		Irregular verbs	
learn → learn**ed**	love → lov**ed**	do → **did**	have → **had**
visit → visit**ed**	study → stud**ied**	go → **went**	hit → **hit**

A **Complete the texts with the simple past of the verbs in the box.**

arrive ~~be~~ hate miss not remember walk want

I remember my first day of school. It [1] ___was___ just horrible! I [2] ________ every minute of it! My older sister [3] ________ with me, but she [4] ________ the way, so we got lost. Finally, we [5] ________, but we were very late. I really [6] ________ my mom and dad. All day, I just [7] ________ to go home.

5.2 SIMPLE PAST NEGATIVE AND QUESTIONS (page 47)

Simple past negative and questions				
	Affirmative	**Negative**	**Question**	**Short answers**
I / He / She / It / You / We / They	**studied** medicine.	**didn't study** journalism.	**Did** he **study** medicine?	Yes, he **did**. No, she **didn't**.

Information questions	
What did you **study?**	**Why did** she **retire**?
When did they **get** married?	**Who did** you **live** with?
Where did he **come** from?	**How many children did** they **have**?

A **Use the words to write questions about when your partner was a child. Ask and answer the questions in pairs.**

1 What / eat?

____

2 Where / live?

____

3 When / start school?

____

4 What / watch on TV?

____

5 What games / play?

____

6.1 *BE GOING TO* (page 55)

be going to **+ verb**				
	Affirmative	**Negative**	**Question**	**Short answers**
I	**am/'m going to save** money for a new bike.	**am/'m not going to waste** money.	**Am** I **going to save** money?	Yes, I **am**. No, **I'm not**.
He / She / It	**is/'s going to buy** her mom a birthday present at the mall.	**is/'s not going to see** the movie with us.	**Is** she **going to sell** some of her old clothes online?	Yes, she **is**. No, she **isn't**.
You / We / They	**are/'re going to do** a lot today.	**are/'re not going to save** money.	**Are** they **going to shop** online?	Yes, they **are**. No, they **aren't**.

Information questions
Who am I **going to go** shopping with?
What is she **going to buy**?
Where are you **going to meet** them for lunch?

A Complete the sentences with the correct form of *be going to* and one of the verbs in the box.

buy	~~come~~	get married	have	lie down	not have

1 The big sale starts tomorrow. ___Are___ you ___going to come___ with us?
2 I'm tired after all this shopping. I __________ for a while.
3 We met at the grocery store, and fell in love. We __________ in November.
4 I'm working all day Black Friday. I __________ time to buy anything!
5 My brother is buying baby clothes. His wife __________ a baby in three months.
6 You found the car you want already? When __________ you __________ it?

6.2 DETERMINERS (page 57)

Determiners		
Things or people in general	**Specific things or people**	**With pronouns**
All sales clerks are friendly. (= sales clerks in general)	**All (of) the** sales clerks here are friendly. (= the sales clerks in this store specifically)	**All of us/them …**
Most stores have good sales on Black Friday.	**Most of the** stores in town have good sales on Black Friday.	**Most of them …**
Many stores are in shopping malls.	**Many of the** stores in this mall are expensive.	**Many of them …**
Some people don't like shopping.	**Some of the** people in my family don't like shopping.	**Some of us …**
No customers like high prices.	**None of the** customers who shop here like high prices.	**None of us/them …**

A Circle the correct words to complete the sentences.

1 *Many of / Many* the good stores in my town are at the mall.
2 *Most / None* stores have special carts for young children.
3 On the day before a big holiday, *none / all* the lines at the grocery stores are very long.
4 *None of / Some* prices in grocery stores are better at the end of the day.
5 *Many of / None* the stores have sale ads in their windows.

7.1 QUANTIFIERS (page 67)

Count nouns …	Non-count nouns …
have a singular and plural form. chili chilies	do not have a plural form. ~~rices~~ rice
use *a/an* for the singular. a chili	do not use *a/an*. ~~a rice~~ rice
use *some* with plural nouns in affirmative sentences. I'd like **some** chilies.	use *some* in affirmative sentences. I ate **some** rice.
use *any* in negative sentences and questions. Do you have **any** chilies? I don't have **any** chilies.	I didn't eat **any** rice. Did you eat **any** rice?

A **Circle the correct words to complete the sentences.**

1 I eat *a few / a little* chocolate every day.

2 I don't have *many / much* time to cook.

3 I try to eat *some / too much* fruits and vegetables every day.

4 I like *some / a little* spicy dishes, but I don't eat them every day.

5 Too *much / many* sweet things are bad for you.

6 I know how to cook *a lot of / not many* dishes because I love cooking.

B **Are the sentences in exercise A true for you? If not, change them to make them true for you.**

7.2 VERB PATTERNS (page 69)

verb + *to* + verb	**verb + verb + *-ing***
I **prefer to eat** at food trucks.	I usually **can't stand waiting** in line.
I **love to try** new food.	I **don't mind waiting** here.

A **Complete the sentences with the correct form of the verb in parentheses.**

1 My brother can't stand ______________ (be) in the kitchen because he doesn't like the smell of cooking.

2 I'm going to go to the beach next month, so I want ______________ (lose) some weight before then.

3 We love to cook together, so we hope ______________ (open) a restaurant someday!

4 I don't enjoy ______________ (cook) because it takes a lot of time.

5 Don't forget ______________ (give) me your recipe – dinner was delicious.

8.1 *IF* AND *WHEN* (page 77)

Statements
I always stay in a hotel near the airport **when** I travel for work.
If I want to explore the city, I use a good online guidebook.
Questions
When you travel, do you usually go by plane or by train?
Do you take a taxi **if** you're late for work?

!

You can put ***if/when*** at the beginning or in the middle of a sentence, and the meaning doesn't change.

If *I'm late for work, I take a taxi. =*
I take a taxi ***if*** *I'm late for work.*

You can use ***when*** for ***if*** and the meaning doesn't change.

When *I'm late for work, I take a taxi. =*
I take a taxi ***when*** *I'm late for work.*

A **Rewrite the sentences with *if* or *when* in the correct place.**

1 I'm on vacation, I love to go to the beach. (when)

When I'm on vacation, I love to go to the beach.

2 We often go to the park the weather is nice. (if)

____

3 I'm always nervous I travel by plane. (when)

____

4 I can, I always prefer to stay in a modern hotel. (if)

____

8.2 GIVING REASONS USING *TO* AND *FOR* (page 79)

Giving reasons using *to* and *for*		
***to* + verb**		
to have lunch	to take a shower	to catch a bus
***for* + noun**		
for lunch	**for** the experience	**for** a shower
So, João, why are you going to Lima?		
To visit Cuzco. And **for the experience**. It's an amazing trip!		

A **Write *to* or *for* to complete the sentences.**

1 Next weekend I'm going to Lima ________ a job interview.
2 Last week I visited my grandmother ________ interview her for a school project.
3 Tomorrow I'm going shopping ________ some new clothes.
4 I'm meeting my best friend later today ________ talk about our vacation plans.
5 I'm going to the library ________ study. It's too noisy at home!
6 My parents never come to my house ________ special events and celebrations. I always go there.

9.1 COMPARATIVE ADJECTIVES (page 87)

Comparative adjectives	
short adjectives: add ***-er***	cold → cold**er** (than) wet → wet**ter** (than)
adjectives ending in *-y*: ***-y*** → ***-i***, add ***-er***	friendly → friendl**ier** (than)
long adjectives: ***more*** or ***less*** + adjective	important → **more** important (than) → **less** important (than)
irregular adjectives	good → **better** bad → **worse**

A **Use the words to write sentences. Use the comparative form of the adjectives.**

1 She / be / happy / in her new job / in her old one. *She's happier in her new job than in her old one.*
2 She / have / interesting / earrings / me. ________
3 Your new scarf / be / nice / your old one. ________
4 I need a belt / that / be / big / this. ________
5 Your shoes / be / dirty / your shirt. ________
6 He is / tall / his father / now! ________

9.2 SUPERLATIVE ADJECTIVES (page 89)

Superlative adjectives	
short adjectives: add ***-est***	young → the young**est**
adjectives ending in *-y*: ***-y*** → ***-i***, add ***-est***	funny → the funn**iest**
long adjectives: ***most*** + adjective	important → the **most** important
irregular adjectives	good → the **best** bad → the **worst**

A **Complete these fun facts with the superlative form of the adjectives in parentheses.**

1 The world's ______________ (long) mustache is more than four meters long.
2 There is an international competition for the world's ______________ (good) beard and mustache.
3 The ______________ (big) hole in a pierced ear is 127 millimeters wide.
4 The ______________ (expensive) earrings in the world cost $57.4 million.
5 An Indian man holds the world record for pulling the ______________ (heavy) things with his beard.

10.1 *HAVE TO* (page 99)

have to **+ verb**

	Affirmative	Negative	Question	Short answers
I / You / We / They	**have to clean** the desks.	**don't have to eat** in the lunchroom.	**Do** you **have to eat** at your desk?	Yes, you **do**. No, you **don't**.
He / She / It	**has to be** very clear.	**doesn't have to stay** outside.	**Does** it **have to be** so loud in here?	Yes, it **does**. No, it **doesn't**.

A **Complete the sentences with the correct form of** ***have to*** **or a short answer.**

1 A How many classes *do you have to go* (you go) to each week?
B I ______________ (go) to my English class three times a week.
2 A ______________ (you work) in the evenings or on weekends?
B No, we ______________ . But sometimes we ______________ (study) for tests then.
3 A ______________ (you give) your homework to your teacher online?
B No, I ______________ . But I ______________ (hand it in) on time!
4 A ______________ (your teacher correct) all your work?
B Yes, she ______________ . She ______________ (do) a lot of work outside of class.

10.2 MAKING PREDICTIONS (page 101)

Making predictions

	Affirmative	Negative	Question	Short answers
I / He / She / It / You / We / They	**will / 'll** **might** **catch** a cold. **may**	**will not / won't catch** a cold.	**Will** you **be** OK?	Yes, I **will**. No, I **won't**.

A **Write the words in the correct order to make sentences.**

1 A college / finish / soon / you / Will
______________ ?
B finish / I / might / this / year
______________ .
2 A after / do / graduate / What / will / you / you
______________ ?
B an / become / engineer / I / 'll / probably
______________ .
3 A boyfriend / get / married / to / Will / you / your
______________ ?

> **!** **When you aren't sure, you can use** ***possibly*** **or** ***probably*** **before the main verb.**
> *You'll* ***probably*** *feel stressed.*
> *You'll* ***possibly*** *feel stressed.*
> **You can also use** ***maybe*** **at the beginning of the sentence.**
> ***Maybe*** *I'll go out with friends after work.*

B get / 'll / married / Maybe / in a few years / we

______________________________.

4 A do / 'll / retire / think / When / you / you

______________________________?

B be / before / I'm / won't / 65 / It

______________________________.

11.1 PRESENT PREFECT FOR EXPERIENCE (page 109)

Present perfect

We use the present perfect to talk about experiences.

We form the present perfect with *have/has* + past participle.

For regular verbs, the past participle looks the same as the simple past (played, called). See the inside of the back cover for a list of irregular verbs.

	Affirmative	Negative	Question	Short answers
I / You / We / They	**have/'ve changed** my password.	**haven't changed** my password.	**Have** you (ever) **joined** a group.	Yes, I **have**. No, we **haven't**.
He / She / It	**has/'s joined** a group.	**hasn't changed** his password.	**Has** it (ever) **snowed** in July?	Yes, it **has**. No, it **hasn't**.

A **Complete the conversations in the present perfect.**

> **!** ***ever** = any time up to now*
> *Have you **ever** seen snow?*
> ***never** = not ever*
> *I've **never** been to Peru.*

1 A I [1] ______ never ______ (add) anyone as a friend on social media, but 200 people [2] ______ (add) me. [3] ______ you ever ______ (add) someone as a friend?

B No, I [4] ______, because I [5] ______ never ______ (open) a social media account.

2 A [6] ______ you ever ______ (build) a website?

B Yes, I [7] ______. I [8] ______ (build) three websites!

3 A I [9] ______ never ______ (change) my password.

B That's dangerous!

11.2 PRESENT PERFECT AND SIMPLE PAST (page 111)

Present perfect and simple past

Use the present perfect to talk about past experiences when you don't specify when they happened.
Use the simple past to say exactly when something happened.

Questions	Answers
Have you ever been to China.	Yes, I have.
When did you go there?	I went last year.
I've never posted a video on social media. Have you?	Oh, yes. I've posted videos lots of times.

A **Read the sentences and write the present perfect or simple past of the verb in parentheses.**

1 A This morning, I ______ (make) a video of myself singing. I want to upload it to my social media page, but I ______ (never do) that before. Can you help me?

B Ask Ryan. He ______ (upload) lots of videos. I ______ (never make) a video before.

2 A ________________ (ever feel) lonely when you're at school, far away from your family?
B Sure. I really ________________ (miss) my mom yesterday, so I ________________ (call) her.

3 A I'm going to eat at Marcella's downtown tonight.
B Really? ________________ (see) the prices on their menu?
A No. I ________________ (go) online yesterday and ________________ (search) for nice local restaurants. ________________ (you eat) there before?
B No, never. It's really expensive.

12.1 QUESTIONS WITH *BE LIKE* (page 119)

Questions with *be like*		
Use questions with *what* + *be* + noun + *like* to ask for a description of something.		
Simple present	What**'s** the weather **like**?	It's cold and windy.
Simple past	**What was** the party **like**?	It was great!
Future	**What will** the course **be like**?	It'll be hard work!

A **Write the words in the correct order to make questions.**

1 like / was / what / the / music / ? ________________
2 what / like / new / 's / their / house / ? ________________
3 was / father / what / his / like / ? ________________
4 food / the / like / be / what / will / ? ________________
5 the / like / was / movie / what / ? ________________
6 will / like / test / the / be / what / ? ________________

12.2 RELATIVE PRONOUNS: *WHO, WHICH, THAT* (page 121)

Relative pronouns: *who, which, that*		
Use *who*, *which*, and *that* to introduce new information about a person or object.		
Use *who* and *that* for people.	I know the people **who** live there.	I know the people **that** live there.
Use *which* and *that* for things.	I like the plants **that** grow there.	I like the plants **which** grow there.

A **Combine the two sentences using *who, which,* or *that*. Make any other changes that are needed.**

1 I live in an apartment. My apartment is near the park.
I live in an apartment that is near the park.
2 There are mountains in the north. They have snow on them all year.
____
3 He works at the ski school. It is in the mountains near here.
____
4 Those are my neighbors. They live in the house next door to us.
____
5 This is the house on the coast. We rented it last year.
____
6 These are my friends from college. They came with us to the concert.
____

VOCABULARY PRACTICE

1.1 PEOPLE YOU KNOW (page 2)

A **Put the words into the right category.**

boss, boyfriend, classmate, close friend, couple, girlfriend, grandchildren, granddaughter, grandson, neighbor, roommate

Family	Work or school	Close or romantic	Where you live

B **Complete the sentences with the correct form of the words from exercise A.**

1 She is not my sister. She is my brother's ________________ . They are in love.

2 My grandfather has five other ________________ : my two sisters and my three cousins.

3 Kevin and Paola are my ________________ at the language school. They're also a ________________ , but they're not married.

4 Fiona and I are ________________ from work. We do a lot of things together in our free time.

5 Isabel is only 45, but she is already a grandmother. Her ________________ , Jazmin, is two years old. She is the daughter of Isabel's son, Oscar.

6 I have a job in a restaurant, and my ________________ is also my ________________ . My apartment is #302. He is in apartment #304.

7 I have two ________________ . We each have one bedroom in the apartment, but we share the kitchen.

1.2 NAMING EVERYDAY THINGS (page 4)

A **Check (✓) the words that you can see in the pictures.**

1 

2 

3 

4 

5 

6 

- ☐ candy bar
- ☐ hand lotion
- ☐ umbrella
- ☐ cash
- ☐ keychain
- ☐ water bottle
- ☐ driver's license
- ☐ mirror
- ☐ gum
- ☐ receipt
- ☐ hairbrush
- ☐ tissues

B **Circle the correct words to complete the sentences.**

1 There is a photo of me on my *driver's license / mirror*.

2 My *cash / water bottle* is empty.

3 Here is the *tissues / receipt* from the restaurant.

4 Do you want a piece of my *candy bar / hairbrush*?

5 Oh, no! It's raining, and my *hand lotion / umbrella* is broken.

6 I need to clean my sunglasses. Will you give me those *tissues / keychains*, please?

2.1 EXPRESSIONS WITH *DO*, *HAVE*, AND *MAKE* (page 12)

A **Circle the correct words to complete the sentences.**

1 I *do / have / make* a lot of work on my laptop every day.
2 I want to *do / have / make* a party when we *do / have / make* some free time.
3 I usually *do / have / make* the dishes, but I don't *do / have / make* other housework.
4 I always *do / have / make* a snack after I *do / have / make* one hour of homework.
5 I want to *do / have / make* plans with some friends, maybe just *do / have / make* something to drink after class.

B **Complete the sentences with the correct *do, have,* or *make* phrase.**

1 Lots of men don't ___do housework___, but not my sons. They ______ after they wake up, and they ______ when their clothes are dirty.
2 Can we ______ now? I'm hungry.
3 I'm tired of walking. I want to stop and ______ at that café.
4 I want to ______ for my birthday party. Can you help me organize it?
5 I always ______ after dinner. I like the kitchen to be clean before I go to bed.
6 Let's go to the movies when you ______ – maybe this weekend!

2.2 NAMING WORK AND STUDY ITEMS (page 14)

A **Match the words on the left to the words on the right to make phrases. Then write full sentences using the phrases.**

(1) a page from	(a) a calendar
(2) music	(b) a textbook
(3) a laptop	(c) files
(4) take	(d) notes
(5) the date on	(e) screen

(6) wear	(f) a document
(7) a computer	(g) headphones
(8) a power	(h) keyboard
(9) read	(i) outlet
(10) free	(j) Wi-Fi

I'm reading a page from my textbook.

B **Circle the correct words to complete the questions. Then ask a partner.**

1 Does your school have good *document / Wi-Fi* and enough *screens / outlets* for all the students' computers?
2 Do you like to listen to music with or without your *headphones / keyboard*?
3 Can you always find your *documents / mouse* and *files / Wi-Fi* on your computer?
4 Do you write important things on your *calendar / keyboard*?
5 Which can you do faster, write *files / notes* with a pen and paper or type them on a *keyboard / mouse*?

3.1 SPORTS (page 22)

A **Circle the correct words to complete the sentences.**

1 Our *coach / court* is happy because we're *losing / winning*.
2 Our *fans / team* is *losing / winning* the game. This is terrible!
3 The *field / players* are walking onto the *court / pool* now.
4 Our town has a new *coach / pool*. It's next to the tennis *players / courts*.
5 Hundreds of *fans / team* are running onto the *field / pool*.

B Complete the sentences with the correct form of a word from exercise A.

1 The first ________ to ________ the FIFA World Cup was Uruguay.
2 An Olympic swimming ________ is 50 meters long, and a basketball ________ is 92 meters long.
3 The soccer ________ is giving instructions. He's at the side of the ________.
4 This place is huge! It has seats for more than 100,000 ________.
5 The ________ on my local team are not professionals, and they aren't very good – they often ________ games.

3.2 EXERCISING (page 25)

A **Match the verbs in the box to the words that can follow them.**

climb	jump	lie down	lift	push
sit down	stand up	stretch	throw	~~turn~~

1 turn around / your head
2 ________ a ball / a paper plane
3 ________ someone away / an elevator button
4 ________ a mountain / stairs
5 ________ a box / weights
6 ________ to rest / on the floor
7 ________ at your desk / in front of the TV
8 ________ your legs before you run / to reach something high up
9 ________ into the water / up and down
10 ________ from your desk / straight

B **Complete the sentences with a word from exercise A.**

1 A good baseball player can ________ a ball more than 130 meters.
2 Some people can ________ more than 6 meters on a trampoline.
3 Some people can ________ 200 kilograms.
4 A very good dancer can ________ a full circle in the air twice.
5 Most people need two months to ________ Mount Everest.
6 For some exercises, you need to ________ on the floor.
7 Before you play any sports, it's important to ________ your arms and legs.

4.1 DESCRIBING POP CULTURE (page 34)

A **Some of the words in bold are not correct. Write in the correct words.**

1 My sister is a **singer** in a ~~**musician**~~ band. They're playing a **concert** tonight.
2 My favorite **TV show** is coming back soon. I love the main **director** in it – he's so funny!
3 Do you know about this new **festival**? It's fantastic! I'm playing it eight hours a day!
4 The **actor** who paints these pictures is very famous. I saw her work at an **concert** in Paris.

B **Complete the stories with the words in the box.**

bands	concerts	festival	musicians

Every year in my town we have a three-day music [1] __________. There are [2] __________ every night, and all the [3] __________ play until late. The [4] __________ are all local people, and everybody in the town goes to see them. Would you like to come with me this year?

actor	artist	director	show	singer	video

My family is very artistic. My mom is a great [5] __________ – she sings in a band. My uncle is an [6] __________. He's starring in a cool TV [7] __________ right now. My brother is an [8] __________. He does the graphics for lots of [9] __________ games. And my dad's a movie [10] __________. He makes great movies. I'm the only one who isn't artistic, but I'm the manager for all my relatives!

4.2 NAMING GIFT ITEMS (page 36)

A **What gift is best for each person?**

candy	gift card	jewelry	purse	speakers	sweatshirt

1 I want something beautiful to wear to parties. __________
2 I prefer to buy my own present in the store. __________
3 I'd like something to wear at the gym. __________
4 I'd like something nice to keep my things in. __________
5 I like music. __________
6 I love sweet things to eat. __________

B **Circle the correct words to complete the sentences.**

1 My grandma likes gifts that she can eat, so I usually make a cake or buy some *flowers / candy* for her.
2 My mom really needs GPS when she drives, but that uses a lot of battery power. So I'm getting her *speakers / a phone charger* for her car.
3 My dad loves sports clothes, so I'm buying him a *sweatshirt / purse*.
4 My best friend loves books, but I don't know which ones she likes. I'm getting her a *purse / gift card* for the bookstore so she can choose.
5 I don't know what to get for my boss for her birthday, so I'm sending her *a bouquet of flowers / jewelry*.

5.1 DESCRIBING OPINIONS AND FEELINGS (page 45)

A Replace the emoji in each sentence with the correct adjective.

1 My first day in college was really *horrible* . I felt very alone, and I missed my parents.
2 My 18th birthday was an ________ experience – for the first time, I was an adult!
3 I remember the first day I went skiing. It was really ________ . My friends and I had a great time.
4 The first time that I voted was a very ________ moment for me. It was an important day for my country, and I was part of it.
5 I remember when I traveled by plane for the first time. That was ________ ! Wow!

B Complete the conversations with the words from the box. Write two more conversations using other words from the box.

angry cool crazy dangerous loud perfect tired

1 **A** How are you feeling today?
B I'm really ________ . I went to bed very late last night.
2 **A** Do you like this music?
B What? I can't hear you. It's really ________ !
3 **A** How was your vacation?
B It was ________ ! The weather was great, and the food was delicious.
4 **A** ________
B ________
5 **A** ________
B ________

5.2 DESCRIBING LIFE EVENTS (page 46)

A Complete the sentences with the correct word or phrase from the box.

buy a house or apartment	get married	graduate from college
learn to drive	meet your future husband/wife	retire

1 These days, people often ________ quite late, when they are 30 or 40 years old.
2 Today, it's important to ________ because you have more choices for work.
3 Some people ________ at the usual time (around age 65), but some work until they are 75 or older.
4 Some young people don't have the money to ________ right away. They stay with their parents until they have enough money.
5 You can't really plan when to ________ . One day, it just happens – you just find the right person.

B **Circle the <u>best</u> phrase to complete the sentences.**

1 My mother has three children, and someday she really wants to *become a grandparent / have a baby.*

2 If you want to *buy a car / learn to drive*, you need to *get a job / get married* and save some money first.

3 My little brother *had a baby / was born* when I was seven, so I helped take care of him. He was so cute!

4 For some jobs, you have to *graduate from college / start school.*

5 She *got married / met her future husband* at the coffee shop where she worked. He got coffee there every day just to talk to her. After they *got married / bought a car*, he told her that he doesn't like coffee.

6 My sister's son *started school / were born* last year, so she has some free time now. She wants to *get a job / retire* soon.

6.1 USING MONEY (page 54)

A **Circle the correct word to complete the sentences.**

1 David wants to buy a car, so he *saves / spends* a lot of his money.

2 Jamelia is very careful. She never *wastes / sells* money on silly things.

3 My friend wants to *spend / borrow* some money from me.

4 I don't like to buy things in stores because it's more fun to *lend / shop* online.

5 Be careful! That phone *costs / pays back* a lot of money!

6 Our store always *borrows / sells* a lot on Black Friday.

B **Complete the questions with the correct form of a verb from exercise A.**

1 Excuse me, how much does this ________________ ?

2 Can I ________________ $2.00? I have $10, but I need $12 for the ticket.

3 Where do you like to ________________ online?

4 This charger was a gift, but it doesn't work. Can I ________________ it without the receipt?

5 If you have enough money, can you ________________ me $20? I'll pay you back.

6.2 SHOPPING (page 56)

A **Complete the shopping words.**

1 c __ __ __ re __ __ __ ter

2 c __ stom __ rs

3 gro __ ery st __ r __

4 dep __ rtm __ nt st __ r __

5 she __ __

6 s __ l __

7 pri __ e

8 salesp __ rson

9 ch __ ck __ __ t

10 c __ r __

B **Complete the text with words from exercise A.**

Last week, I went to a new [1] ________________ store to buy some milk. It was in the back. I needed to walk down many aisles. In one aisle, they had a really good [2] ________________ on bottled water, so I decided to buy some. In another aisle, there was some delicious bread. There was some very interesting fruit, fresh fish, and delicious rice in other aisles. Next to the milk, there were amazing cheeses! I walked down most of the aisles in the store. When I got to the [3] ________________ , my [4] ________________ was full. There were three [5] ________________ in front of me. I waited and read a magazine from the [6] ________________ . Then I decided to buy it, too.

7.1 NAMING FOOD (page 66)

A Complete the text with the words in the box.

avocado	~~cereal~~	jam	lettuce
peanut butter	salmon	strawberries	yogurt

My daily food diary

Saturday

A bowl of [1] ___cereal___ for **breakfast**, I just love granola!

Lunch with friends, a salad with [2] ________ and [3] ________, and fruit for dessert: some fresh [4] ________. Delicious!

At home, I make toast with [5] ________ and [6] ________ for the kids. They love that **snack** combination!

For dinner, we have [7] ________ with green vegetables. It's good to eat fish once a week. Then [8] ________ with honey for dessert – simple but healthy.

B Circle the correct word to complete the sentences.

1 I like *yogurt / chili* without sugar for breakfast.
2 I'm vegetarian, so I don't eat *burgers / avocados*.
3 I like a lot of *yogurt / onions* on my pizza.
4 I make corn with just butter, *salt / strawberries,* and pepper. Very simple, but very good.
5 Some people like bread with butter for breakfast, but many people like to put *cereal / jam* on it, too.

7.2 DESCRIBING FOOD (page 68)

A Match the two parts to make a complete idea.

1 Doctors say that raw vegetables are … ___
2 This chocolate is delicious! ___
3 That coffee is very bitter. ___
4 I live by the sea … ___
5 My favorite food isn't very healthy. ___
6 Thailand, Mexico, and India … ___

a I think it needs some sugar.
b Can I have another piece, please?
c good for your body.
d so we always have a lot of fresh fish to eat.
e It's a fried peanut butter sandwich with jam on top!
f are famous for their spicy food!

B Complete the sentences from the conversations with the food words in the box.

boiled	delicious	fried	grilled	raw	roasted	sour	spicy

1 If you have a bad stomach, don't eat too much [1] ________ food like curry or chili. Just some [2] ________ rice and chicken – and drink plenty of water.
2 What about today's special? It's really [3] ________. Everybody loves it!
3 How would you like your fish, sir – [4] ________ over an open fire or [5] ________ in olive oil?
4 Can you cook this meat a little more? It's still [6] ________.
5 Don't eat that yogurt! It smells very [7] ________ to me. I think it's bad.
6 We normally eat [8] ________ meat in my country. We cook it in the oven for a long time so it is very easy to eat.

8.1 TRAVELING (page 76)

A Look at the words in the box. Find words that mean …

airplane	backpack	bus station	check-in counter	guidebook
map	suitcase	tour bus	tour guide	tourists

1 two places where you begin or end a trip: ________ ________
2 two objects that give you information about a city: ________ ________
3 people who are on vacation: ________
4 a person who takes you to interesting sights when you're on vacation: ________
5 two kinds of luggage: ________ ________

B Use the correct form of the words in the box in exercise A to complete the sentences. Use each word or phrase only one time.

1 Last time I went to the airport, it was awful. I arrived very late, and there was a long line at the ________ .
2 We live near the airport, so we often see ________ in the sky over our house.
3 When I go on vacation, I always take two big ________ . One for my clothes and one for the things I buy. My sister doesn't like shopping, so she just brings one large ________ .
4 Last year I worked as a ________ . I worked on a ________ . It left from the central ________ and took people all around the city. The ________ loved it!
5 When I visit a new city, I always buy a local ________ to tell me about the best restaurants. Then I use the ________ on my phone to help me find them!

8.2 USING TRANSPORTATION (page 78)

A Circle the correct verbs to complete the text.

I usually go to work by bus. It takes me about 45 minutes. I leave home at 7:15. I walk two blocks to the bus stop and I [1]*get in / get on* the number 72 bus. The 72 takes me to the park. There, I [2]*pick up / change* buses and take the 35. Sometimes I [3]*miss / catch* the 35, and then I have to wait and [4]*take / miss* the 44. The 35 [5]*gets into / drops me off* right in front of my office. The 44 stops several long blocks away. If it's a nice day, it's OK. I can walk to work from there. If I'm late, I [6]*get onto / get into* a taxi. I get to the office at 8 o'clock.

B Choose the correct verbs from the box and write them in the correct form to complete the texts.

catch	change
drop off	get into
get off	get on
get out of	miss
pick up	take

Group Chat

1 I'm just ________ the taxi. Be there soon.
2 Oh, no! I just ________ my train!
3 I can see her. She's ________ the bus now!
4 I'm ________ Jake's car now. We're on our way.
5 No taxis! I'm ________ the subway. I'm going to be late. Sorry!

Write a message …

9.1 NAMING ACCESSORIES (page 86)

A **Look at the pictures. Make sentences with *He's/She's (not) wearing* and the accessory words in the box.**

He's wearing sunglasses.

belt	bracelet	earring(s)	glove(s)	necklace
scarf	sneakers	sunglasses	tie	

B **Circle the correct words to complete the sentences.**

1 I need a *belt / bracelet / tie*. My pants are too big.

2 My hands are cold. Where are my *gloves / sneakers / socks*?

3 You need a *bracelet / necklace / scarf* in this cold weather.

4 She's wearing *a scarf / sunglasses / a tie*, so I can't see her eyes.

5 I love your *earrings / gloves / socks*. Are they real gold?

9.2 DESCRIBING APPEARANCE (page 88)

A **Look at the words in the box. Choose the correct words to match the descriptions.**

bald	beard	curly	dark	gray
light	mustache	pierced ears	straight	

1 the hair on your face: ____________________

2 what you have if you wear earrings: ____________________

3 a way to describe a head without hair on it: ____________________

4 ways to describe hair color: ____________________

5 ways to describe how hair looks: ____________________

B **Complete the sentences with words from exercise A. You won't need all of the words.**

1 Do most people in your family have dark or ____________ hair?

2 I don't wear earrings because I don't have ____________ .

3 Does he have a mustache and a ____________ ?

4 My father is completely ____________ , but all my brothers have a lot of hair.

5 Is her hair straight or ____________ ?

6 One of my grandmothers has normal ____________ hair, but my other grandmother colors her hair bright red!

10.1 DESCRIBING JOBS (page 98)

A **Circle the best words to complete the sentences.**

1 Wow! That's an amazing building. Who was the *photographer / architect*?
2 My sister is a *call center worker / nurse*. She spends all day on the phone.
3 I have a problem with my car. I need to call *an engineer / a mechanic*.
4 The *receptionist / police officer* recommended the hotel restaurant.
5 Lie down and relax. The *photographer / nurse* said you need to rest.
6 I asked a *call center worker / police officer* to help when somebody took my purse.

B **Match the jobs to the things people say.**

accountant	dentist	IT specialist	lawyer
paramedic	physical therapist	project manager	

1 ______ "My client, Mr. Gaston, did not steal the money."
2 ______ "Give all your receipts to me. I manage the business's money."
3 ______ "Sorry, but I think you have a software problem."
4 ______ "OK, now carefully stretch out your left leg. Good!"
5 ______ "The work has to be completed by April 10. We're on schedule."
6 ______ "Open your mouth wide, please."
7 ______ "Now we're going to take you to the hospital."

10.2 DESCRIBING HEALTH PROBLEMS (page 100)

A **Circle the correct verbs to complete the phrases for injuries and illnesses.**

1 *break / catch* a cold
2 *break / get* your leg
3 *catch / have* a sore throat
4 *catch / hurt* the flu
5 *cut / have* a stomachache
6 *cut / have* a toothache
7 *cut / have* your finger
8 *break / bang* your head
9 *feel / have* a fever
10 *hurt / cut* yourself shaving
11 *get / hurt* your back
12 *have / hurt* a headache
13 *catch / twist* your ankle

B **Complete the sentences using a phrase from exercise A. For some sentences, there is more than one possible answer. Make sure to use the right form of the verbs and pronouns that fit the sentences.**

1 Did you ______ in a skiing accident?
2 Don't ______ with that knife!
3 Go to the dentist if you ______ .
4 I ______ because I ate too much.
5 I ______ because of the loud music.
6 People often ______ when they have a cold or the flu.
7 You ______ . It's 39.4 degrees!
8 There was blood on his shirt because he ______ .

11.1 USING VERB-NOUN INTERNET PHRASES (page 108)

A **Match the ten phrases to the definitions.**

1 add someone as a friend	**2** build a website	**3** change your password
4 check your messages	**5** click on a link	**6** join a group
7 make a video	**8** message someone	**9** open a social media account
10 swipe left or right		

a press the mouse on text to go to a website ___
b move the screen to one side or the other ___
c record and edit live action ___
d see if you have any new email or texts ___
e create your online identity ___
f contact someone by electronic text ___
g make a new internet destination ___
h choose a different security code ___
i include another person in your network ___
j become a member ___

B **Circle the best phrases to complete the sentences.**

1 I never *check my messages / build websites* on a computer. I just use my phone.
2 In some apps, to show that you like something, you can *swipe right / message someone*.
3 Oh, no! I *clicked a link / joined a group*, and now my computer has a virus.
4 I like my boss, but I don't want to *add her as a friend / open an account for her* on social media.
5 At my office we have to *change our passwords / make videos* every six months. It's important to be safe.

11.2 USING SOCIAL MEDIA VERBS (page 111)

A **Replace the icon with a verb from the box. Which of these sentences are true for you? Tell a partner.**

download	go viral	like	search for	share

1 I usually _______________  photos of my friends.
2 I love to watch cat videos, and I _______________  them on social media with my friends.
3 I _______________  lots of videos, but I don't have time to see them all.
4 If some of my videos _______________ , I'll be so happy! I want everyone to see my work.
5 I sometimes _______________  information about Australia. I really want to visit there someday.

B **Complete the sentences with the correct verb from the box. Are the sentences true for you? Change them if they are not.**

block	bookmark	follow	log in	upload

1 To see "My Account" information on my bank's website, I have to _______________ with my username and password.
2 I _______________ people on social media if they post things I don't want to see.
3 I _______________ lots of famous people on social media. I like to know what they're doing.
4 I have my own website, and I _______________ my videos there so other people can enjoy them.
5 If I go online and find a site that I like, I always _______________ it so I don't lose it.

12.1 DESCRIBING WEATHER (page 118)

A **Look at the pictures. Which weather words from the box do you associate with the pictures?**

blizzard	boiling	cloudy	drought	flood
foggy	freezing	humid	hurricane	rainy
snowstorm	snowy	sunny	thunder and lightning	windy

1 Picture A: ________________

2 Picture B: ________________

3 Picture C: ________________

4 Picture D: ________________

5 Picture E: ________________

B **Replace the weather symbols with the correct words.**

The weather today is warm and [1] ________________, with the maximum temperature of 23°C. But it's going to be [2] ________________ in the morning and [3] ________________ in the afternoon. We might even get some [4] ________________ in the evening, and it'll be very [5] ________________ all day. If we get a lot of rain, we may have a [6] ________________, so be extra careful if you're driving!

Write a message …

Brrr, it's [7] ________________ out there today, so wear your warmest clothes. Later on this evening, we can expect to get a [8] ________________ that will last all night. Tomorrow will continue to be [9] ________________, so stay home if you can.

Write a message …

12.2 DESCRIBING LANDSCAPES AND CITYSCAPES (page 120)

A **Look at the map. Find ten of the features from the box on the map. Label them.**

1 cave
2 cliff
3 coast
4 fountain
5 glacier
6 rainforest
7 rocks
8 statue
9 tower
10 waterfall

B **Choose the best word to complete the texts.**

1 It's a beautiful place on the *coast / glacier*. There's a big wide beach at the foot of a tall *field / cliff*. There are some *valleys / caves* there also, so you can keep out of the sun when it's too hot.

2 Downtown there are some tall *skyscrapers / waterfalls* and a big open square with a *fountain / cave* in the middle. It's a great place to go in the evening to hang out with friends.

PROGRESS CHECK

Can you do these things? Check (✓) what you can do. Then write your answers in your notebook.

UNIT 1

Now I can …	Prove it
☐ use words to talk about the people in my life.	Write two family words, two words for people you work or study with, and four other words for people you know.
☐ talk about the connections between the people in my life.	Write about someone you know and what connection that person has to other people you know using possessive adjectives (*my, our, his*, etc.).
☐ use words for everyday objects.	Write four things you have with you today and two things you always have in your bag.
☐ talk about what belongs to me and to others.	Look around the room and write three sentences about objects and who they belong to. Use possessive pronouns (*mine, ours, his*, etc.).
☐ start a conversation with someone new.	Write three ways to start a conversation.
☐ write a formal email of introduction.	Look at your email from lesson 1.4, exercise 2D. Can you make it better? Find three ways.

UNIT 2

Now I can …	Prove it
☐ use expressions with *do*, *have*, and *make*.	Write five things related to activities at home. Use *do*, *have*, and *make*.
☐ talk about what I do every day, on the weekend, etc.	Write five things you do regularly (every day, every week, etc.).
☐ use words for work and study.	Write a description of the place you do your work and/or schoolwork.
☐ use *this/that one*; *these/those ones* to talk about things.	Complete the sentences: *I don't like these shirts. I prefer* ____________ *over there.* *That car is OK, but* ____________ *is much nicer.*
☐ describe communication problems and how to fix them.	Write two ways to explain a communication problem and two ways to check the problem.
☐ write your opinion and give information in an online comment.	Look at your comment from lesson 2.4, exercise 3C. Can you make it better? Find three ways.

UNIT 3

Now I can …	Prove it
☐ use words to talk about sports.	Write two verbs for sports, three places for sports, and five other sports words.
☐ talk about what I am doing now.	Write one thing you're doing at the moment and one thing you're not doing at the moment.
☐ use words to describe exercise.	Write five verbs to describe exercise.
☐ talk about what I do every day and what I'm doing at the moment.	Complete these sentences: *I usually …* *At the moment, I …*
☐ ask for information.	Write two ways to ask for the price of a soccer ticket.
☐ write a short comment about positives and negatives	Look at your comment from lesson 3.4, exercise 1E. Can you make it better? Find three ways.

PROGRESS CHECK

Can you do these things? Check (✓) what you can do. Then write your answers in your notebook.

UNIT 4

Now I can …	Prove it
☐ use words to talk about pop culture.	Write five jobs, two special events, and three other words about pop culture.
☐ talk about plans.	Write two things you're planning to do on the weekend. Use the present continuous.
☐ use words to talk about gifts.	Write three gifts you can wear, two you can use, and one you can eat.
☐ use *him*, *her*, etc. to talk about people and things.	Complete these sentences with an object pronoun: *Soccer is his favorite sport. I love … , too.* *Their parents always give … money for their birthdays.*
☐ make and respond to invitations.	Write one way to make an invitation and one way to accept an invitation.
☐ write an event announcement.	Look at your event announcement from lesson 4.4, exercise 3D. Can you make it better? Find three ways.

UNIT 5

Now I can …	Prove it
☐ use words to talk about feelings and opinions.	Write five positive words, three negative words, and two words that can be positive or negative.
☐ talk about events and people in my life.	Write three things you did last year.
☐ talk about life stages.	Write six life stages in the order that they usually happen.
☐ ask questions about people's lives and say what they didn't do.	Complete the sentences: ________ he retire last year? No, he ________ .
☐ congratulate and sympathize with people.	Write two ways to congratulate someone and two ways to sympathize with someone.
☐ write an online comment agreeing or disagreeing with someone.	Look at your comment from lesson 5.4, exercise 2D. Can you make it better? Find three ways.

UNIT 6

Now I can …	Prove it
☐ use verbs to talk about money.	Write three verbs that go with *money*, two verbs that go with *things*, and three other money verbs.
☐ talk about future plans.	Write about a plan you have for next week and a plan you have for next year. Use *be going to*.
☐ use words to talk about shopping.	Write three places for shopping and four things you can find in a store.
☐ talk about quantities of things.	Complete the sentences: *Many of the stores in my town don't … All department stores sell …*
☐ say what I want when I do not know the word.	Think about something you want to buy but you don't know the word for in English. Write a short conversation in a store. Explain what you want.
☐ write a vlog script.	Look at your vlog script from lesson 6.4, exercise 3E. Can you make it better? Find three ways.

PROGRESS CHECK

Can you do these things? Check (✓) what you can do. Then write your answers in your notebook.

UNIT 7

Now I can …	Prove it
☐ use food words.	Write three count and five non-count food words.
☐ talk about quantities.	Write about the quantities of different kinds of food you eat every week. Use *a little, a few, a lot of,* etc.
☐ use adjectives to describe food.	Write five adjectives for preparing food and five adjectives for flavor.
☐ talk about what I like to do.	Complete the sentences about food with a verb + *to* + verb, or a verb + verb + *-ing*. *I would like …* *I enjoy …*
☐ order food in a restaurant.	Write one expression a customer uses and one expression a server uses in a restaurant.
☐ give my opinion in an online comment.	Look at your comment from lesson 7.4, exercise 2E. Can you make it better? Find three ways.

UNIT 8

Now I can …	Prove it
☐ use words to talk about traveling	Write two kinds of luggage, two places you travel from, and six other vacation words.
☐ talk about travel and vacation preferences.	Complete these sentences: *When I'm on vacation, I usually …* *If I can, I always …*
☐ use verbs to talk about transportation and trips.	Write five verbs you can use with *bus* or *train*.
☐ talk about reasons.	Write three reasons why you're learning English. Use *to* or *for*.
☐ make suggestions and give advice.	Write two ways to suggest a plan for this evening.
☐ give advice in a short comment.	Look at your comment from lesson 8.4, exercise 3D. Can you make it better? Find three ways.

UNIT 9

Now I can …	Prove it
☐ use words for fashion accessories.	Write two accessories you wear on your feet, two accessories you wear around your neck, and five other accessories.
☐ compare two things, people, or places.	Write sentences to compare these two pairs of things: sneakers/socks New York/my hometown
☐ use words to describe a person's face and hair.	Write two words for hair on the face and three words to describe hair.
☐ compare two or more different things, people, or places.	Complete this sentence: *The* ____________ *(good) place to take pictures in my city is …*
☐ ask for and give opinions.	Write one way of asking for an opinion and one way of giving an opinion.
☐ write a paragraph about an image.	Look at your paragraph from lesson 9.4, exercise 2D. Can you make it better? Find three ways.

PROGRESS CHECK

Can you do these things? Check (✓) what you can do. Then write your answers in your notebook.

UNIT 10

Now I can …	Prove it
☐ use words for jobs.	Write two dangerous jobs, two office jobs, and four other jobs.
☐ talk about things that are necessary.	Write one thing you have to do and one thing you don't have to do in this class.
☐ use words for health problems.	Write two phrases for different accidents, two ways you feel when you get sick, and two other health problems.
☐ make predictions	Complete these predictions: *One day I'll …* *I probably won't …* *Next year I might …*
☐ ask for and offer help.	Write three different ways of asking about a problem.
☐ write an email giving advice.	Look at your email from lesson 10.4, exercise 2C. Can you make it better? Find three ways.

UNIT 11

Now I can …	Prove it
☐ use phrases to talk about the internet	Write six phrases for things you can do on the internet.
☐ talk about experiences	Write about an experience you've had and one you haven't had.
☐ use verbs to talk about social media	Write three verbs you can use with *videos* and two verbs you can use with *people.*
☐ talk about experiences and give more information.	Write about something exciting you've done. When did you do it?
☐ make and respond to requests.	Write one way to make a request and one way to respond to a request.
☐ write a comment about an infographic.	Look at your comment from lesson 11.4, exercise 2D. Can you make it better? Find three ways.

UNIT 12

Now I can …	Prove it
☐ use words to describe weather	Write three words to describe hot weather, three words to describe cold weather, and three words to describe wet weather.
☐ ask questions with *be like.*	Complete the sentences: *What* ________ *the festival* ________ *last week? What* ________ *the weather* ________ *tomorrow?*
☐ use words to describe landscapes	Write two words to describe the landscape near your home, two landscape features that you can't find near your town, and two other landscape features you like.
☐ use *who, which,* and *that* to give more information about people and objects.	Complete these sentences: *She's the woman who …* *That's the picture which …* *This is the beach that …*
☐ ask for and give directions.	Write two different ways to ask for directions. Write three different ways to give directions.
☐ write a simple set of instructions.	Look at your instructions from lesson 12.4, exercise 3D. Can you make them better? Find three ways.

PAIR WORK PRACTICE (STUDENT A)

2.3 EXERCISE 4 STUDENT A

Choose a reason for calling from the list below. Think about what you want to say, and add some detail. Now phone your partner. Use the chart below to help you.

Reasons for calling

- you're sick
- there's a problem with the subway, and you're late
- you want to meet
- you have a problem you want to talk about

Student A		**Student B**
Greet B and give a reason for the call.	→	Greet A. Tell A there's a problem.
Try to solve the problem. Ask if it's OK now.	→	It isn't OK now. Ask A for repetition.
Repeat what you said.	→	The problem continues. Suggest a solution.

3.3 EXERCISE 2D STUDENT A

1 **Ask Student B some questions about the items below using the functional language on page 26. If B doesn't understand the word, explain it with the definitions in parentheses.**

The restroom (*where the public bathrooms are*)

The bleachers (*the cheap seats in a stadium that aren't covered*)

A side of fries (*some fries with your food order*)

2 **Now listen to Student B. If you don't understand a word or words, repeat them as a question. Do you understand the words now?**

5.3 EXERCISE 2C STUDENT A

1 **Tell your partner what good things happened yesterday. Use these words:**

graduated new job house / apartment car

2 **Now listen to the good things that happened to student B. Congratulate him/her, but check the information he/she gives you*, and offer the correct version using *Do you mean …?* or *You mean …?***

*(*Clue: Use the Vocabulary words on page 46 to check.)*

5.5 EXERCISE B GROUP A

Story A

Eva Hart from the U.K. was only seven years old. She traveled as a second-class passenger with her parents. Her father put Eva and her mother on a lifeboat. He didn't survive. In later years, Eva was very critical of the shipping company – The White Star Line. After the accident, she even wrote an autobiography, *Shadow of the Titanic, A Survivor's Story*.

PAIR WORK PRACTICE

5.5 EXERCISE B GROUP B

Story B

Molly Brown was a 44-year-old American woman. She was a well-known politician from a rich family. She traveled alone as a first-class passenger. She escaped the sinking ship on a lifeboat. She helped a lot of the survivors on board the *Carpathia*. She became famous because of her bravery and spoke a lot about the tragedy in the years to come.

6.3 EXERCISE 4 STUDENT A

1 **You want to buy something from a drugstore but you don't know the word for it in English. Choose one of the objects below and ask the salesperson for what you want.**

A 

B 

C 

D 

E 

2 **You are now the sales clerk. Your partner wants to buy something. Begin by asking if you can help.**

7.3 EXERCISE 2D STUDENT A

Situation 1

Imagine you're in a restaurant. Ask the waiter what he recommends. You're a pescetarian (you eat fish but not meat). Use *I mean* to be clear about what you eat and what you don't eat.

Situation 2

Imagine you're a waiter in a restaurant. Ask if the customer would like dessert. Recommend the strawberry cheesecake. Now recommend the fruit salad. Yes, there are a few strawberries in the fruit salad.

8.3 EXERCISE 2C STUDENT A

1 **Ask student B for some suggestions for what to do when you have free time in a city. Listen and respond. Use an echo question if necessary.**

2 **Give student B some advice using the suggestions below:**

Go to the mall with a group of friends. It's only half an hour by car.

Have something to eat at a local café (please use the name of a real local café). It's pretty cheap and has good food.

Go to the movies. There's a great movie playing now that won an Academy Award, and it starts at 8:30 p.m.

11.3 EXERCISE 2D STUDENT A

1 **Complete the sentences with a question from the Real-world strategy box. Then ask your partner.**

1 When your phone has no power. ______________________ it?

2 Those black and white pictures on the page. You use your phone to read them. What ______________________ ?

3 The person who invented cell phones. What ______________________ ?

2 **Now listen to your partner. Answer their questions with one of these answers:**

It's called "**international roaming.**" They're called **SIM cards.** You **upload** it.

PAIR WORK PRACTICE

2.3 EXERCISE 4 STUDENT B

Choose a communication problem from the list below. Think about what you want to say. Now wait for your partner to phone you.

Communication problems

- echo on the line
- bad connection
- traffic or a train noise
- problem with the Wi-Fi

Student A		Student B
Greet B and give a reason for the call.	→	Greet A. Tell A there's a problem.
Try to solve the problem. Ask if it's OK now.	→	It isn't OK now. Ask A for repetition.
Repeat what you said.	→	The problem continues. Suggest a solution.

3.3 EXERCISE 2D STUDENT B

1 **Listen to Student A. If you don't understand a word or words, repeat them as a question. Do you understand the words now?**

2 **Now ask Student A some questions about the items below using the functional language on page 26. If A doesn't understand the word, explain it with the definitions in parentheses.**

The parking lot (*where you park your car*)

Baseball cap (*the hat baseball players and fans wear*)

A noise maker (*something you use to make lots of noise in the game*)

5.3 EXERCISE 2C STUDENT B

1 **Listen to the good things that happened to student A. Congratulate him/her, but check the information he/she gives you*, and offer the correct version using *Do you mean … ?* or *You mean … ?***

*(*Clue: Use the Vocabulary words on page 46 to check.)*

2 **Now tell your partner what good things happened yesterday. Use these words:**

baby moved future husband / wife college

5.5 EXERCISE B GROUP C

Story C

Carla Jensen was a 19-year-old young woman from Denmark who worked as a servant. She traveled with her brother, uncle, and fiancé. They didn't have much money, so they traveled third class. They wanted to live in the U.S., but only Carla survived. Her family put her into the lifeboat because women went first. After the accident, she returned to Denmark and never left her country again.

PAIR WORK PRACTICE

5.5 EXERCISE B GROUP D

Story D

Charles Joughin, from the U.K., was 32 years old. He worked as a baker on the Titanic. He was one of the 212 crew members who survived. To escape, he jumped into the water and swam to a lifeboat. The water was very cold! The people on the lifeboat saw him and rescued him just in time. He became famous after the accident because of his amazing escape.

6.3 EXERCISE 4 STUDENT B

1 **You want to buy something but you don't know the word for it in English. Choose one of the objects below and ask the salesperson for what you want.**

A

B

C

D

E

2 **You are now the salesperson. Your partner wants to buy something. Begin by asking if you can help.**

7.3 EXERCISE 2D STUDENT B

Situation 1

Imagine you're a waiter in a restaurant. Ask if the customer would like to order now. Recommend the chicken. Then recommend the beef.

Situation 2

Imagine you're in a restaurant and you would like to order dessert. Ask the waiter what he recommends. You're allergic to strawberries (you can't eat any strawberries). Use *I mean* to be clear about what you can and can't eat.

8.3 EXERCISE 2C STUDENT B

1 **Give student A some advice using the suggestions or ideas of your own.**

Visit the local museum. It's only $5.00 per person and has a really interesting section on local history.

Go shopping for souvenirs. Stores open at 9:30 a.m., and there's a sale.

Rent a bike. It's a really cheap way to see the city, and there's a docking station a block from your hotel.

2 **Ask student A for some suggestions for what to do after class today. Listen and respond. Use an echo question if necessary.**

11.3 EXERCISE 2D STUDENT B

1 **Listen to your partner. Answer his/her questions with one of these answers:**

His name is Martin Cooper. They're **QR codes**. You say "my phone's dead."

2 **Now complete the sentences with a question from the Real-world strategy box. Then ask your partner.**

1 When you want to put a photo on a social media site. What ________________ ?

2 Those things in your phone that hold data. What ________________ ?

3 When you use your phone in another country. ________________ it?